AFTER EXILE

AFTER EXILE

A Raymond Knister Reader

Edited and Introduced by

Gregory Betts

Library and Archives Canada Cataloguing in Publication

Knister, Raymond, 1899-1932
    After exile : a Raymond Knister poetry reader / edited and introduced by
Gregory Betts.

Poems.
Includes bibliographical references.
ISBN 978-1-55096-228-4

    I. Betts, Gregory, 1975-   II. Title.   III. Title: Raymond Knister reader.

PS8521.N75A17 2011   C811'.52   C2011-907130-4

Design and Composition by Hourglass Angels-mc
Typeset in Palatino at the Moons of Jupiter Studios
Printed by Imprimerie Gauvin

Published by Exile Editions Ltd.
144483 Southgate Road 14 – GD
Holstein, Ontario, N0G 2A0
Canada   www.ExileEditions.com
Printed and Bound in Canada in 2011

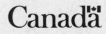

Conseil des Arts   Canada Council
du Canada   for the Arts

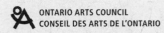

Canadä

ONTARIO ARTS COUNCIL
CONSEIL DES ARTS DE L'ONTARIO

The publisher would like to acknowledge the financial support of the Canada
Council for the Arts, the Government of Canada through the Canada Book
Fund (CBF), and the Ontario Arts Council–an agency of the Government of
Ontario, for our publishing activities.

Sales / Distribution:
Independent Publishers Group
814 North Franklin Street, Chicago, IL 60610 USA
www.ipgbook.com   toll free: 1 800 888 4741

"He that observeth the wind shall not sow;
and he that regardeth the clouds shall not reap."
– *Book of Ecclesiastes*, Chapter 11.4 –

Contents

Introduction

In 1931, one year before Raymond Knister accidentally drowned in Lake St. Clair, the acclaimed poet, novelist, and short-fiction author was forced, once again, to confront his economic instability, and the inevitable difficulties of making a living as a professional writer in Canada. The horizons of possibilities were bleak by any estimation, even more so for writers like he with avant-garde literary and aesthetic ambitions. He also had a family complete with newborn baby to support and Toronto was bogged down suffering through the Great Depression. Writers across the country commiserated each other with glooms of their own, offering advice and words of encouragement. Novelist and short-story writer Marcus Adeney wrote to Knister, "The lemon may be a dry one but squeezing is probably better than using a hammer" (3.7.1931). Morley Callaghan offered his friend some murky words of comfort: "You are right; everybody is having difficulty, and the one comforting thought is that things can't get any worse" (11.11.1931).

Knister died in the lake at Stoney Point the next summer: young and bristling with potential. In the year between his death and Callaghan's cold solace, Knister's life went through an emotional and geographic roller-coaster that saw him in the bustle of Toronto to the "sifting and floating" of rural Ontario farm life (see "The Hawk"), from the blossoming cultural intensity of Montréal to the soft lakeshore of Canada's southern tip. He spent a lot of time writing a novel, tucked away in the quiet of Port Dover. He spent even more time travelling, following employment opportunities, searching for wherever the Canadian literary scene was happening.

In a convergence of personal and professional disappointments, in 1931, his father, whom he was particularly close with, died, while Toronto's arts community was stuck in an awkward mid-Depression transition. Knister wasn't sure he wanted to stay. Budgets were tighter and the atmosphere, as A.J.M. Smith described it, a tad superciliously, was stifling.

Knister's reputation has grown since his premature death for his short stories, novels, and poetry (see the list of poetry anthologies on page 195). In Robert Lecker's 1995 list of the most-anthologized Canadian writers, that includes fiction, Knister ranks 23rd overall — beating the likes of Robertson Davies, Emily Carr, and A.M. Klein: Morley Callaghan places first on the list (Lecker, *Making It Real*, 143). In the development of our literary history, Knister has been labelled a "farmer who was also poet" (the title of a CBC radio special on him), and described as a "rural writer" too many times to note. There is no question or doubt that Knister's particular genius lay in the "soundless horizon" of the country (from "The Hawk"), and that much of his life involved his family's Ontarian farm. But Knister's rural background has been meticulously explored and documented by many critics to the general exclusion of the other geographies of his life. It is simply false to imagine or construct Knister as an isolated literate in a culturally smitten environment: Knister was very much involved in various urban literary environments actively developing modernist aesthetics and method. In his brief 16-odd years as a writer, Knister participated in arts communities in Toronto, Montréal, Chicago, and Iowa City for extended periods. He was also frequently in Detroit, the closest city to his father's farm, and New York.

The influence of the modernist literary world on his writing has been well documented. His poetic style has been fairly compared to T.S. Eliot, Ezra Pound, Rainer Maria Rilke, and William Carlos Williams, all of whom he read and admired. His rural verse was also (favourably) compared to work by Robert Frost, Carl Sandburg, Edwin Ford Piper, and Edgar Lee Masters, all of whom he read, admired, *and* personally met. But Knister was not just soaking up the lessons and achievements of English-language poets around the globe: he was part of a field of artists in Canada struggling to connect the new ideas to their "new" country. His peers and companions in this country included novelists like Marcus Adeney, Morley Callaghan and Frederick Philip Grove, short story writers Walter Imrie, Tom Murtha, and D.C. Scott, playwrights like Merrill Denison, Fred Jacob, and Roy Mitchell, and poets like Florence (and her daughter Dorothy) Livesay, Leo Kennedy, and Edward Sapir. Though it has been generally understated in literary histories since, for most of Knister's life Toronto was the centre of a distinctly Canadian modernism struggling to emerge — and he was at the centre of Toronto's arts community.

Being the axis of the country's manufacturing and banking industries, 28 October 1929 hit Toronto hard. It burst — or contributed to the burst of — the burgeoning modernist bubble that had been growing in Toronto throughout the 1920s; a modernism that was lush with the optimism of aesthetic renovation, national rejuvenation, and participation in the global initiative. Knister was a prominent figure amongst those filled with the jubilant mood of untapped possibilities. At various times, living in Toronto were recognizable literary figures like the writers mentioned above, as well as

Ernest Hemingway, Wyndham Lewis, Arthur Stringer and Frank Prewett. W.B. Yeats came to visit at least twice to lecture and help develop Merrill Dennison and Roy Mitchell's modernist theatre. Other notable lecturers passed through regularly, such as self-proclaimed "half-Canadian" Nobel Laureate Sinclair Lewis (who eccentrically claimed popular writer Harvey O'Higgins as his favourite Canadian author one trip, then Morley Callaghan the next), Emma Goldman, Siegfried Sassoon, and many others. The Arts and Letters Club had its own series of regular speakers, discussion groups, performances, and various stage antics to challenge, provoke, or merely entertain local intellectuals. The members of the Group of Seven, and their partisans across the city, province, and country, were pioneering a Canadian style of modern painting, triggering debates on style, form, and the importance of *the nation*. Toronto, led by Lawren Harris, was, in fact, only one of three North American cities interested enough in the avant-garde to attempt a massively expensive exhibition of works of modernist painters like Picasso, Duchamp, Kandinsky, Miro, and Man Ray, amongst hundreds of other visual artists. The exhibition, in 1927, set attendance records at The Art Gallery of Toronto, and was by any standard a triumphant success (see Ruth Bohan's *The Société Anonyme's Brooklyn Exhibition* for further details of the American event, *Catalogue of the International Exhibition of Modern Art*, and Sybille Pantazzi's "Foreign Art at the Canadian National Exhibition 1905-1938" for details of the show in Canada). Katherine Dreier of New York's Société Anonyme lectured on the modern arts to packed halls. Modernist ballerina, Saida Gerrard, arrived in Toronto during this period, as well as a B.C. painter, Emily Carr, who spent a month meeting and greeting artists about town, rejuvenating her own career through the encouragement of those she met.

Adding to momentum of the period, Knister published an anthology of Canadian short fiction in 1928, the first of its kind, pushing writers with a noticeably modernist aesthetic. The book led A.J.M. Smith to wonder, "Is it too much to hope that it may be one of the heralds of the renascence that seems just over the edge of the horizon[?]" (11.8.1928).

And finally, to round out this perfunctory survey, Winnipeg's Bertram Brooker had long established himself in the city and was exhibiting strange and occultic abstract paintings, while passing around twisted, surrealist poetry to friends he admired. Brooker published his manifesto-esque "When We Rise!" in an important arts survey in 1929 promulgating the surge of the movement and its oppositional forces. Brooker was concurrently writing a novel that would eventually win Canada's first Governor General's Award for Fiction (in 1936), producing surrealist plays for Hart House (first staged in 1932), and painting staggering Kandinsky-esque abstracts. On Knister's last night in Toronto before his death, both he and Knister stayed up late discussing literary ideas and reading Brooker's manuscript of *Think of the Earth* (see page 118). Though this night was a major development in their friendship, it never had the chance to mature.

There were other poets whom we now recognize that were also active in the city at the time; writers like Frank O. Call, W.W.E. Ross, Louise Morey Bowman, and Albert Durrant Watson, and while they may not have been aggressively, or successfully, modernist, they contributed to the promulgation of artistic feeling and interest of those times. Older figures, like Bliss Carman, Charles G.D. Roberts, Wilson

MacDonald, and D.C. Scott, were tolerated but mocked by the new order when their backs were turned. Callaghan and A.J.M. Smith, especially, couldn't understand or tolerate Knister's respectful association with them. Morley asked bluntly, "In any other country in the world they are not taken seriously. Why do you do it? Since you know better… is it the mellowing effect of the soil?" (15.8.1928). Knister refused to let the old guard influence his writing (he savaged Roberts' book *Spring Breaks in Foam* in review, saying "work like this has become as common…. as the art of embroidery was a generation ago" in "Canadian Poems of the Month." February 1927), but considered them respect-worthy men *on a personal level* of a previous literary era. The aesthetic orientation of Toronto had shifted: modernism was being hatched, if tenaciously and stubbornly. Herman Voaden described this era in Canada as "a time of visions" (Voaden, "Earth Song").

Despite the activity, the city was heavily debilitated by the fiscal realities of the publishing industry. Even though it was the heart of the trade in Canada, Toronto was little more than a meagre publishing capital of original literature, most often churning out reprints of confirmed best-sellers from Britain and America. Its very paucity propelled the poets abroad, pushing them to the centres of English Language excellence. Without intending to exaggerate the depth of Canadian modernist experimentation and participation, but in recognition of the general lack of awareness of these contributions, here is a cursory survey of relevant Canadian activity during Knister's lifetime: Florence Livesay published in *Poetry* and *The Dial*; Florence Ayscough collaborated with Amy Lowell in *Fir-Flower Tablets* (1922); Louise Morey Bowman published in *Voices*; Edward Sapir (whom Knister declared in a letter to Harriet Monroe to be "our best litter-ateur" 5.3.1926) published regularly in *The Dial*, *Poetry*, *The Nation*, *The New Republic*, *American Mercury*, and *Language*; Arthur Stringer, a literary celebrity across North America, published widely across the continent, including over a hundred-page book of free verse; Frank Prewett (nicknamed "Toronto") published two volumes of verse with Virginia Woolf's Hogarth Press; W.W.E. Ross published in *The Dial*, *Poetry*, and *New Directions*; and Tom Murtha, Knister's pro-tegé and friend, worked and published with *The Midland*. Morley Callaghan and Mazo de la Roche, though not poets, published in *This Quarter*, *transition*, and many others. All the Toronto writers of substance also published in *The Canadian Magazine*, *The Canadian Forum*, *Saturday Night*, the *Toronto Daily Star*, Toronto's *The Star Weekly*, and *Willison's Monthly*, none of which paid enough, nor evaluated strictly enough to take too terribly seriously.

Knister's own work appeared in *Voices*, *Poetry*, *The Mid-land*, and *This Quarter*. There was enough happening in the city, and in the province, to lend to it the feel of a potential renaissance: somehow always — *tragically* — just around the corner. Callaghan ran a money-losing lending library down the street from *Saturday Night* headquarters that Knister would visit regularly, sometimes weekly. They discussed books and what it would take to launch Canadian litera-ture, evaluating who had potential and who were the writ-ing dead. Other artists and writers would drop in and join, borrow a book or not, and leave. Knister's enthusiasm led him to write to editors like Sir John Willison (*Willison's Monthly*) and Harry Moore (*Canadian Stories*), and alter-nately encourage them to publish "the most individually

Canadian" work (15.6.1925), or chastising them for failing that challenge. "My notion of such a magazine," Knister wrote to Moore, "runs to some such motto as Canadianism at all costs. Too many stories have got into our magazines which might have been written anywhere. If the public gets to know that what you supply them is as Canadian as maple syrup, they'll come for it. And when it comes to subjects, it seems to me that Canadian farm life has long and sorely been neglected" (8.2.1928).

It should be noted that Knister's nationalism does not contradict his modernist aesthetic, but was in fact, a general and important characteristic of the particular transitional modernist aesthetic in Toronto at the time. Unlike Americans, Britons, or Europeans, in general, Canadians did not feel that their national identity necessarily opposed their art, but rather considered Canada's emerging society as a rare opportunity to shape it by their own ideology (Brooker's "When We Rise!", Harris' "Revelation of Art in Canada," or Voaden's "Creed for a New Theatre," for instance).

Henry Adaskin, the well-praised violinist of the Hart House Quartet, who often socialized in the apartment building where Knister's future wife Myrtle, along with Wilson MacDonald, Charles G.D. Roberts, and numerous other artists lived, describes his perception of the period:

> All the greatest [musical] performers of the world, Caruso, Ysaÿe, Kreisler, Heifetz, Chaliapin, Casals, and many others came to Toronto time and time again. There was hardly a great artist anywhere in the world who didn't appear in Toronto at some time… It was during those eight years at the Hambourg Conservatory, from 1928 to 1936,

that we really got to know the artists' community of Toronto, although some of them we had met a few years before. The sculptors Mani and Betty Hahn I already knew from the days of Fran's flat in 1923. Soon after, I became acquainted with Lawren Harris, Bertram Brooker, Alec Jackson, Bess and Fred Housser, Arthur Lismer, Charles and Louise Comfort, Will Ogilvie, Fred Varley, Emily Carr, Gordon Davies, the sculptors Florence Wyle and Frances Loring, Bobs and Peter Haworth, and a great many other, younger artists, like Tom Stone, Lowrie Warrener, Yvonne Mc-Kague, Isobel McLaughlin, and Gordon Webber.

A few of these became my lifelong friends. What I learned about art from Mani, and even more so from Betty Hahn, formed my taste and outlook for the rest of my life. This was helped by a fortunate policy of the Toronto Art Gallery; all through those years it undertook, through the generous financial help of private citizens, to bring in exhibitions of the works of a great number of the then avant garde artists of the world. Arts works which have become historical points of reference, like Duchamp's "Nude Descending a Staircase," or Brancusi's "Bird in Flight," or the melted watches of Dali, all were shown in Toronto at that time, as well as innumerable works by Cézanne, Matisse, Van Gogh, Picasso, Braque, Klee, Schwitters, Gaugiun, Chagall, Modigliani, Arp, and many, many others. It was an education in itself. (141, 149-50)

The emerging portrait of an active, almost *vibrant*, arts community in Toronto significantly contrasts with Montréal-based scholar Ken Norris' presumption that Knister and the only three other poets he considers noteworthy (R.K. Everson, W.W.E. Ross, and Dorothy Livesay) were nothing but "individual and unrelated" (Norris, 11). He justifies his dismissive assertion with a quote from Montréal's Louis Dudek, and the terse explanation that their "poems appeared in American and English literary publications" (Norris, 11) — as if publishing abroad was enough to discredit all Canadian modernist experimentation before things shifted to Montréal. In a much better evaluation of the period and its poetry, David Arnason refers to Knister's era as "a period of inter-regnum... Each [of the poets he discusses] is aware of, and part of the evolution of modern poetry as an international phenomena; yet each is peculiarly Canadian" (Arnason, "Canadian Poetry: The Interregnum," 28). His thoughtful consideration of Louise Morey Bowman, Lawren Harris, W.W.E. Ross, and Raymond Knister, however, remains limited to the literary world without recognizing that these advanced writers were working amidst similarly numbered modernist artists across "the seven arts" ("The Seven Arts" was the title of Brooker's weekly, nationally syndicated column for Southam newspapers on the state of Canadian culture). Knister's assessment of himself (see page 186) suggests both his experimentation and interdisciplinary approach as reasons for his obscurity: the same could be said for most of the artists of the period. And while taking a multidisciplinary perspective on the period may not change its overall assessment, it will at least shift the perception of period from "inter-regnum" to the verge of a movement.

Within the Toronto artistic community, and beyond, Knister was quickly recognized as a vibrant new voice. His verse disseminated across North America, also appearing in *The American Mercury, The Buccaneer, American Poetry Magazine, The Farmer's Advocate, The New Outlook,* and University of Toronto's *The Rebel,* on top of all the journals already listed above — and all this during his short lifetime. His short fiction, it should be noted, spread even faster and farther, his novels were considered literary events, and he also had a one-act play published by *Poet Lore* in 1928. The poems, to which we limit ourselves in this context, were notably compared by Herbert Read in T.S. Eliot's *The New Criterion* as being refreshingly objective and masculine compared to less successful writing by the likes of James Joyce, Richard Aldington, Ernest Hemingway, William Carlos Williams, amongst others Read dismissed (*New Criterion* 1925).

Toronto's modernist initiative burst shortly after Black Monday, though the economic loss only slightly heightened the financial straits of the artists of the period. Given the swirl of activity, it is an intriguing sociological mystery — too broad for this context — to consider all the great variety of ideological, aesthetic, financial, and colonial factors that prevented the arts community from propelling forward into the rich aesthetic initiatives it promised. Harris left. Brooker stopped painting. Callaghan left. Roy Mitchell had already gone. Everything seemed to shift to Montréal, to New York, to Paris; away. Knister left too.

In "Canadian Literati," written for the *American Mercury* (ultimately rejected by the magazine, but printed in *Poems, Stories, and Essays*), Knister notes a "distinct vibration" coming from the literary youth of Montréal. He moved to Quebec to review the developments first-hand and to meet A.J.M. Smith, A.M. Klein, Leo Kennedy, and the rest of the McGill Group of Poets. He later moved to the MacDonald College campus in Ste. Anne de Bellevue where the little *Canadian Mercury* was publishing. Nothing substantial came of either: Knister was back in Ontario by June of 1932.

The poet had a glimmer of respite from the pan-Canadian financial gloom in 1931 when Frederick Philip Grove wrote to inform him that Knister's second novel *My Star Predominant* had won the Graphic Press annual award for the best Canadian novel. It was the only award of its kind in the country, and certainly the richest. The publisher boasted the prize of $2, 500 (approx. $28, 500 in current currency value) in large paid-advertisements, but their promise of riches died as unsubstantiated as Jacques Cartier's stories of Canadian diamonds. The Ottawa-based publishing house went bankrupt and, though Knister eventually received around half his due, the money only came after mounds of paper and puddles of ink wasted in threats and consultations. In the summer, an embittered Grove, who had been pressured by his employer to volunteer in the contest he found distasteful, and who got personally involved in Knister's defence, buckled under the pressure: "The point is that I have lived in great anxieties lately…. It is now all cut and dried; I am leaving Canada and returning to continental Europe after having wasted forty years of my life here" (25.6.1931).

Despite his interminable reputation as a "farm boy," Knister stopped working on the farm in 1923 and never returned but to visit or to help his father, who died in 1931. In a letter he wrote to himself at age 14, Knister details precisely how he dreamed of leaving the farm and becoming a famous writer. The path to a successful literary career, he wrote, begins with reading and ends without farming. True to his adolescent career vision, Knister became one of Canada's first successful professional writers. The depth of that achievement is enhanced when we consider that he did it without any of the support system writers have today: federal, provincial, and municipal funding; national distribution systems; a Canadian audience interested in Canadian literature; an international audience interested in Canadian literature; over a hundred magazines that pay for poetry (1997 numbers); and over 50 universities and colleges with Creative Writing programmes and Writer-in-Residence positions. Knister, along with most of the literary industry, wrote with no institutional or governmental support. Not only was he fighting the aesthetic and financial barriers caused by a terribly small, pre-modern audience, but he also fought the constantly reinforced limitations of subject matter, of what kind of stories could be told in Canada. He consistently demanded that stories, true, artistic stories, could happen anywhere — especially in the Canadian countryside. The resistance was all too real, and registered all too keenly in his pocketbook. His stories were rejected by J.H. Cranston of the *Toronto Daily Star* for being, in Knister's opinion, "too Canadian." In Knister's lifetime, serious literature happened elsewhere. Cranston advised him, "Humour, of course, is very desirable" (14.10.1925). Pot-boilers, Knister called such financially motivated entertainment pieces. At various times, he begrudgingly wrote and published such pieces under various pen names. Without disrespecting today's writers' hunger for more funding, power, and prestige, Knister's struggle underscores precisely how far we've come as a literary marketplace.

This is why it is so important to recognize Raymond Knister's personal achievement: he, in the midst of economic calamity, in the midst of a country just beginning to respect itself and its artists, lived by writing words that continue to resonate today. The amazing fact of Raymond Knister is that he made it as a writer without having to compromise. He was a professional writer of serious fiction, and, even during the worst economic period in the country's history, he never stopped writing. When he died, things were on the upswing. In 1932, upon returning to Toronto, Knister had earned himself a permanent assistant editor position at Ryerson Press, had finalized the Graphic Press fiasco, had committed to Macmillan to be a paid reader, and was negotiating publications with British and American publishers (two of his novels still linger *tantalizingly* in the archives, unpublished). Leo Kennedy declared that when Knister died, "he was on his way *up*.... Everything was going good for the guy and he knew it. He said it. He wrote it to me" (Kennedy quoted in Givens, *Afterword* 78). On the very morning he died, Myrtle Knister quotes Raymond himself in her diary as saying, "I feel just like Keats did when he was just coming into his powers. I feel as though I am just coming into mine. The world is before us, Myrtle. We have everything we want and we are happy" (reprinted in Givens, "Raymond Knister — Man or Myth?"). The two had a minor argument, and Raymond proposed a swim. He went out alone.

By an uncanny coincidence, the September 1932 issue of *The Canadian Forum* had organized a special feature on Knister as part of their series on Canadian authors, with a critical assessment and a reprint of nine poems. It was to be the first serious attention he had received from his home country, but what had been intended to serve as just recognition tragically became eulogy after 29 August 1932. John B. Lee notes that on 31 August, the day before Knister's body was discovered at the bottom of Lake St. Clair, darkness spread across Canada in an extraordinary solar eclipse.

Included in this collection are a series of letters relating to his death, and to the eventual publication of his poetry in book form. Each of the poetry collections published so far have advanced the study of Knister's verse by presenting new poetry and providing a new context in which to imagine the author. This collection hopes to offer the same: there are many poems, versions of poems, letters, articles, and prose sketches never collected in book form, or, in some cases, never previously published at all. It cannot claim to be a *final* collected edition, as new poems are bound to surface, but it is the closest of such kind to date. This project as a whole functions as a Raymond Knister "Reader" in that it offers all the poems alongside numerous documents with which to peer into the life of the poet and imagine the personal and cultural context in which some of the best verse, prose, and criticism of the period was written.

The title *After Exile* obviously stems from his stereoscopic long poem of the same name. It was written after Knister returned from Chicago and *The Midland* in that rare moment, after he had decided to become a *Canadian* writer, as he confronted the landscape for the first time from this new perspective. Ironically, the poet could only find an American publisher for the poem. In some ways, this poem also registers Knister's new exile in returning to Canada. He was writing in his own country about his own country, but the sharp gaze of his writing eye was too precise for Canadian editors, readers, and professors to accept. The rest of the world was hailing him as a major talent; accolades poured in from everywhere but here. Even his friend, the respected critic William A. Deacon, wrote to say, "I see the pictures, follow your thought, but your words do not sing to me out loud… My feeling is essentially one of indifference because I cannot <u>hear</u> them" (4.6.1924). Unlike the famous exiles then populating Paris and Italy, Knister was, in many ways, an exile in his own country: a Cassandra prophesizing an already existing Canada. Unlike those other modernist expatriates, Knister fought to change the conditions of his exile.

The amazing thing is that Raymond Knister saw through the economic cloud hovering over his life, saw through the disintegration of modernism in Ontario, and saw through the colonial blind cast over the entire country. He knew Canadians weren't ready for his writing — the proof was piled in the rejections slips from every journal and publisher going — but he knew that a literary industry began with eyes that could see the world in a different way. In coming back to Canada, in exchanging forms of exile, he committed himself to the possibility of enabling a substantial literary tradition here.

He died before the end of the interregnum.

Gregory Betts
Hamilton, Ontario

Editor's Note

Despite the fact that Knister wrote less than 120 poems, anthologists have had a difficult time collecting his works. The first "Collected Works" to be published, for instance, contained only 35 poems. Subsequent installations have added poems but missed others without explanation. There are many difficulties in assembling a collection of poetry: sustaining the tug-of-war tension between the author's intentions, historical precision, readability, and scholastic completeness is an almost impossible task. So, be forewarned that this collection does not surmount all these muddy mountain barriers: it is not a variorum edition, it does not answer all questions about Knister and his poetry, its information may need, one day, to be updated, and it clearly violates rules of intentionality by publishing poems the author never submitted in his lifetime.

Given the limitations, however, this collection has much to offer. It is the first reprint of Knister's verse in over 20 years, and represents a major step forward by publishing over a dozen poems for the first time in book form, and printing over 30 poems and variations, on top of numerous letters and prose pieces, for the first time ever. All bibliographic information aspires to completeness but recognizes the improbability of total closure. To demonstrate the difficulty, an article appeared not too long ago in a non-national newspaper by writer Marty Gervais about a mysterious woman dropping off "prose and poetry manuscripts" by Raymond Knister. I was able to corroborate that these poems were in fact copies of previously published work, but who knows how many other mystery women are out there and what they have in their possession?

Careful readers will note minor changes in a few poems; changes that are limited to standardizing spelling or "quietly" correcting obvious typos. For example, Knister published "The Ploughman" in *The Midland* in 1922, but the title was changed to "The Plowman" in *The Canadian Forum* in its 1932 feature on Knister. All subsequent reprints bore the latter moniker. For since Knister's handwritten manuscript and his subsequent notes refer to the poem as "The Ploughman," however, the Canadian spelling has been restored. Similar unobtrusive editorial adjustments have been made in only a few of the poems and prose selections.

Dates and locations listed most often indicate Knister's mailing address at the time he typeset or rewrote that particular version of the poem. Most of the poems exist in many different versions, and as Knister very infrequently dated his writing, what dates are included were taken from his notes and manuscripts, and, most often, posthumous additions by the research and memory of Myrtle Grace (nee Knister) and Imogen Givens. Many thanks must be extended to them both for their care in protecting the great masses of Knister papers for over half a century, and for their tireless work cataloguing and meticulously documenting Knister's work.

All sketches were done by the hand of Myrtle Grace, except for the one on page 140 which was done by Kay Folk. Collages were assembled, variously, by Myrtle and the editor. All poems, photographs, sketches, and letters have been reprinted with the kind permission of the copyright holder, Imogen Givens.

Acknowledgements

Ray Ellenwood, Barry Callaghan, Carl Spadoni, Thomas-Fisher Rare Books Library (University of Toronto), United Church Archives (University of Toronto), Victoria Archives (University of Toronto), York University Archives, Queen's University Archives, University of Western Ontario Archives, and Ted Betts. Most of all, I'd like to thank Lisa for her endless and inspiring encouragement and support. Many thanks to the staff at the William Ready Archives (McMaster University) — the heart of Knister studies and the most friendly and courteous archive and research environment I encountered. Special thanks to Imogen Givens for supporting and fostering this project with such enthusiasm.

"Spring finds me with exile's fever,
and I am thinking of return."

— Raymond Knister, 14 May 1924,
Letter to William Deacon. Iowa City, Iowa —

Grass * Plaitings

Collection selected by Raymond Knister and sent to Lorne Pierce in 1925 but was unpublished in his lifetime.

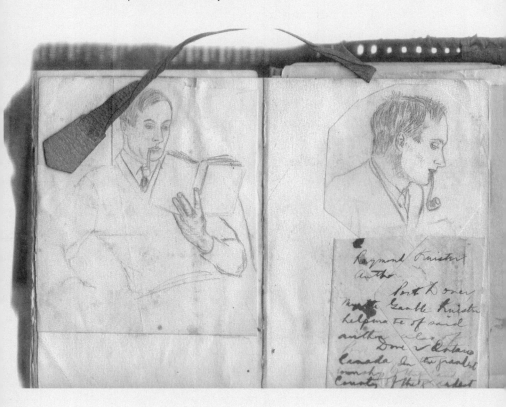

A Road

Summer

A white-hot, endless-seeming streak.
Motors advance and recede
With level swiftness,
Dulling and shining,
To leave a swirl of dust,
A scent of perfume and cigars.
Puffing tractors pull two wagon-loads
Of wheat to mill.
Funerals go by with brisk sedateness,
Then to return,
Swift, bunched and scattered,
With joyous whoop of siren...
Boys tossing and brandishing light dinner-pails:
Agile-fingered drumming...
Trucks of vegetables and loads of hay
Meet and pass.
Low rich level land on either hand,
Fields of muddy-green and amber,
Of tobacco, beans, wheat, corn;
Orchards, blue-green and red-green
Of apples and peaches.
Houses vivid, barns light-grey...
In the after-day
Looking toward it and the sunset
A coral dust-mist rises,
Above, around the whirr of motors...
Dusk. Couples' talk in rare open buggies.

Autumn

A dull brown road, and deep.
Wagons with bags and humped or recumbent men,
Top-buggies, "democrats" of farmers,
Flivvers, – hardy perennials –
Twisting and tolling.
Threshing-outfits, their palsied lumbering roll and hissing
To a belated clover-hulling...
Fields tarnished, sodden, or faded,
Or green-streaked with new wheat,
Or with furrows notching the sky-line.
Houses drab, dull, dreary in rain,
Barns four-square in dejection,
Muddy-grey, roofs dirty-green.
A wedding, people happy, sensing change;
Raised to reality – a dream now
Their ends-for-means existence,
The scrabblings in soil
And mean sorrows and satisfactions...
Evening, resonant air, the "plunk-plash" of a horse
Along the lonely thick way;
Swift trillings of bird-song, broad-cast sown,
Beauty and dreariness,
Blossoms and sodden soil,
Silence, chill.

Winter

A dead-white writhing way.
Canals through the snow-banks,
Only the breath-mist of a horse showing
Above the ridges.
Pitch-holes and cutter-tippings.
Sleigh-loads of pig-feed,
By times of tobacco
Wending to market...
Moonlight, a livid and ghastly world,
With jealously watching
High-wrought trees,
Roaring, tentacular,
Sighing and furry trees,
Houses, with sparks of little lights, strands of smoke,
Infinitely tiny, inappraisably lonely
From the Road.

December 1920.

Cedars

Do you remember
How that night the cedars
Gloomed blue and vagabond-sturdy in moonlight,
Moonlight changing the air to frost,
And they held themselves erect with an effort
And muttered and sighed and chanted
In inebriate frenzy,
And leaned to each other with maudlin sobs?
The moon looked down but would not see them.

Them we shall remember
When our strivings have long been loud in the world,
When we reel through action and glory
And think with our shoutings to shatter
The mist and the frost of the void.
When we quiet our clamour, and, awaiting the echo,
Choke for the air, and it is not, and mocks us,
And our head sinks down and we cannot raise it,
Holding our hand behind us, hoping that life may come and take it yet;
And the soul floats high, and will not see,
Cannot even smile.

Blenheim, Ontario.

5

Lake Harvest

Down on the flat of the lake
Out on the slate and the green,
Spotting the border of Erie's sleeping robe of silver-blue changeable silk,
In sight of the shimmer of silver-blue changeable silk,
In the sun,
The men are sawing the frosted crystal.
Patient the horses look on from the sleighs,
Patient the trees, down from the bank, darkly ignoring the sun.
Each saw sings and whines in a grey-mittened hand,
And diamonds and pieces of a hundred rainbows are strewn around.

February's Forgotten Mitts

Shep lies long-bodied upon the auburn grass –
It has been dried in the glance of the sudden sun.
As you pass he wrinkles a sideward eye to the astounding blue of heaven.
Half a mile away the year's first cackling of hens, aroused from the cold.
The boughs of the elm and maple wait, expectant.
The fields and roads rejoice in slithering mud over the frost.

Somewhere a well-clear, golden echo of children's voices crying and calling.
After dinner Pete looks around for his mitts.
He has lost them about the barn this morning:
Spring has flung forward an unringed hand.

Peach Buds

As we wait
In the dark,
In Winter's young Spring-rain
Stricken the lashed drops cling.

In dawn, in the wind
We crispen,
Complaining silverly,
Weeping.

The sun makes fire
With our silver
Over the valley
An hour
As we wait.

Child Dreams

The boy lies dreaming,
Dreaming, asleep
In the deep bed.
He rides high on a golden chariot
Through a still golden world...

But now the wheels are squeaking,
Dolefully clacking and squeaking.
The golden world is changed to verdigris,
And writhes
In the squeaking
Endless
Of his chariot wheels.

He starts awake to sun-held morning,
The cries, ceaseless,
Of blackbirds in trees.
Through the windows
Wide curtains sweep outward
Flaunting and beckoning:
Young air,
The smell of changing sod.

Black-birds
Dark in the clutched boughs,
Burnished copper in illimitable haze of light
Squeak ceaseless
Dolefully
Squeak.

Martyrdom

Brown leaves are hurried
(recalcitrant swiftness!)
For all their clutching
Of grass and moulder
Soiled in rain-pools of yesterday.

Others happier
Far more happy
Winged suddenly
High lifted,
Crucified on the wires,
Swing and writhe
Transfixed on thorns
In immeasurable pain,
Immeasurable ecstasy.

Night Walk

Wind, and the dark, and the cool
Momently, lightly, beat forth.
The cricket shrills.

The wind, so fleet, so gentle,
Erratically so steady,
Makes titillation
In leaves unseen:
Rythmic, almost imperceptible
Ebb and flow among the pines,
Is the ceaseless, unabashed caressing
Heard by inland beaches
Of the inconstant wave.

Nearer, the used eye may see
Tall pines jostling
In mock sedateness
Against the near-black sky.

Ungraspable odour is the air
That haunts,
Reminds of itself.

My soul is steeped in calm.
Then,
Like the sudden unprompted
Chant of a bird
When all the woods
Are still,

I am drawn to cognizance
Of the myriads of men everywhere
Dumbly, unconsideringly striving
To shape their lives,
Asleep now.

August 1919. Blenheim, Ontario.

Feed

For Danny whistling slowly
"Down in Tennessee"
A fat white shoat by the trough
Lifts his snout a moment to hear,
Among the guzzling and slavering comrades,
Squeezing and forcing:
And begins to feed again.
Whenever the certain note comes
He will raise his jaws
With his unturning eyes,
Then lean again to scoop up the swill.

The Spirit of War

She is in the air of chambers
Where foregather one or two
Drunk with wine and a fear
That the world heeds them
In not the right way.
She is in the mind of the munition-inventor,
Maddeningly inconsequential,
Never-sated;
Attends and stands between at the meetings of kings;
At idle-courts and idler camps she is mistress of the revels
But that is too small a realm for her:
She is in the illimitable flare
Of fear-born hate and exiguous rage
Having for mother fear of the need for pity
Of self, of others.
And when the hate gives out
She makes of it for man a game:
"Just to *show you* what it means
To rouse me:"
And he kills himself by the year,
By the million.

The cries of choked drownings, of wailing shell
With swishing eviscerations,
Of crashing planes are music
To charm her – but not to sleep:
Sight of a million slain,
Earth's horses and earth's men,

Heaving their bellies to the soulless sky,
The reek of human bodies boiling
To make cartridge-grease
Of a million lives runted
From too much sacrifice
Is perfume;
But she faints not,
Nor stifles from satiety.

Presently the million tumuli are over-greened.
Nature forgets:
Holds nothing against man:
Besides, for his own undoing
Suffice himself
And, ever-evocable, his, the Spirit,
Abundantly.

8 January 1921

Reverie: The Orchard on the Slope

Thin ridges of land unploughed
Along the tree-rows
Covered with long cream grasses
Wind-torn.
Brown sand between them,
Blue boughs above.

. . . .

Row and row of waves ever
In the breaking;
Ever in arching and convulsed
Imminence;
Roll of muddy sea between;
Low clouds down-pressing
And pallid and streaming rain

December 1920. Blenheim, Ontario.

As a free flowing dream, it appears to move from what is observed in the first stanza to what is dreamed in the second. However, the actual transition from "reality" to "illusion" or "dream" is never really entered into. Rather it is presented as a "fait accompli," as a transfiguration continually occurring. The actual process of transfiguration, therefore, must occur in the reader's mind as he or she connects the poem's two independant and yet related pictures.

— *Marcus Waddington*, Thesis. *171-2.*

The Wind

The wind is not punily consentient;
He romps over prairies and cities,
He loiters in stock-yards and parks,
He noses through barn-yards and flower-beds.
He makes one of bays and the black flats of skyscrapers.

You, as for you the door of your car is opened,
He greets, insistent and blandly aware
As you could wish,
Blithely unmeaning as
On the faces of your savage fathers.

Elm-Tree and Sun

The elm-tree
Is a fan
Half-opened
Plied coquettishly
By the invidious
Fingers of earth
To the inflamed stare
Of the sun,
Shut off, now
And again by the dark lid
Of the clouds.

It draws
And wafts onward
A breath
From the void.

6 January 1921. Blenheim, Ontario.

The Colt

Through the gate
The boy leads him,
Turns him, expectant,
Around;
Slips off the halter:
He whirls, is gone,–
Boy brandishing
The halter at his going,
Clapping his hands–
Unnecessary–
In long lopes he speeds,
Rising and dipping,
Down the rolling lane.
Such beauty, see,
Such grace,
Moving (diversely!)
Never was.
Nor such gait-perfection
And exactness
Is in any man.
His mane and his tail
Lie back on the breeze,
And the breeze at his every lope
Surges past
His laid-back ears.

See the long swift
Flash and swing,
Low,
Of his limbs...
Gone now,
But back streaks his whinny
Wild, enimaging himself;
He will round the gate corner
At the end of the long pasture
With entrancing ease
And speed,
Re-accelerate,
Bound onward to his comrades,
And stop.
Or else, breaking
Into a high free stride,
Trot up to, around them,
Tail up, nose inheld;
Greet his kinsfolk.

The farmer looks over his fence
To see him pass;
And his world,
And its days, make him say:
"Idle colts!
Somehow nohow of any use!"

Blenheim, Ontario

Change

I shall not wonder more, then,
But I shall know.

Leaves change, and birds, flowers,
And after years are still the same.

The sea's breast heaves in sighs to the moon,
But they are moon and sea forever.

As in other times the trees stand tense and lonely,
And spread a hollow moan of other times.

You will be you yourself,
I'll find you more, not else,
For vintage of the woeful years.

The sea breathes, or broods, or loudens,
Is bright or is mist and the end of the world;
And the sea is constant to change.

I shall not wonder more, then,
But I shall know.

11 January 1921

The Quester Rewarded

Man!
You have trailed the spoor of knowledge
From stalactites to shell-holes
From cradle-side to grave-side,
From world-founding to millenium,
From Eden to Utopia,
(Utopia, O resplendant No-man's Land!)
Dream of moths and stars
Dream of madrepore, ichthyosauri,
Of culinary constellations,
Dream of the thoughts of your self,
Of sages' words and the crowding planets
That shut out the Great Outside
Are within you.
Long have you sought
And might have sought and never ceased,
But the most that you can ever know
Is that never can you know all,
That search is the only treasure-trove.
You have riddled your earth
Like a rotten cheese
You have scurried around it,
Millipede-wise,
Thinking perhaps that your momentum
Would hurl you over its round!
Long have you journeyed,
Giving of your sleep and your soul:
But do not despair,

Though you've forgotten the quest which lured you first,
Some day, if you are patient,
You are going to find
Yourself;
You shall have
The matchless line of sky and sea
To consider and to enjoy.

Over Trees and Spring Dusk

Whither the clouds,
Drifting level, merging slowly,
In silence,
From the sunset's purple cave,
Through dolphin-shoals
Athwart the ghost moon-shallop –
Drifting level, merging slowly
To what unseen ports
Or glimmer of simulated dawn?

See alternate version.

Frost in Childhood

Ah, delicate traceries upon the pane,
When have I not wondered before you,
Whether the heavier frost had formed you,
Or whether a flaw in the pane!
Now I see that you are the breath
Within,
Though the greatening outer cold
Make you less delicate and clear
So that I may not see forth, –
Now I can see
That when night brings you no more
The house shall be unpeopled.
The moon gilds you, before the dark room
And the sun of the day shall gild,
Melt you away in drops.

Blenheim, Ontario.

Enemies

YOU ask me for forgiveness.
Would it were you I must forgive,
I that could forgive!

We stood before the lights
In strange garments.
You could have forgotten
But for the inexorable Prompter –
And the mass before us that applauded and egged us on.
It was of It the Playwright had thought,
It I should try to forgive.

"And the powerful play goes on?"
The powerful play goes on;
With guffaws from roof-chandeliers to god-like pit.

Arab King

You hear the seethe of the crowd, Arab King, (as it were from
its beat) about your stall, on the outworn sod across to
the edge of the race-track, from the grandstand, from
within the ring.

Men crowd about your door, breathing their eagerness over
each other's shoulders, looking, in the stable-hands'
silence, and the curses of your jockey.

You look above them all, out to the hidden track, – the dry ditch banked by weedy humans – look, and give the loud wild whinny, that can call no answering, that can be no answering.

Was it a sneak in the night, Arab King, was it some small-hour thug – who dumbs your feet for now, and shrouds the velvet and charged platinum of you in worse than defeat?

The crowd ebbs. Hope cannot die! ... Then the race begins without you. And you raise again your high, straining challenge, that no one hears.

It shakes long in a fierce despair over the crowd-fields as they watch your peers, and long and shrill again.

The hoofs of your peers down the home-stretch come as a splatter of rain-drops upon shingles athwart the hum of stillness. Every drop is ten feet gone, across the dust...

Over the roar of the shouting crowd-field hangs the iron pang of your challenge, to remind them all.

It wrings your inappeasable flanks as you look, as you strain the ropes at either side. There will be no forgetting. Never will anything have the string of this!

Did anyone know? Did anyone understand?

Time

I thought that old earth's flesh was dead,
So panged of cold it lay,
So dried and powdered.
But the sun came strong,
Hid all else but himself,
Bending a strong breath upon it,
'Til moisture came,
And the flesh was freshened
Richly,
To await another dry-time
After the flourish and rise of green,
After the cutting and trampling of yellow.

Stable-Talk

We have sweat our share;
The harrow is caught full of sod-pieces,
The bright discs are misted yellow in the wet.
Hear tardy hesitant drips from the eaves!
Let the rain work now.

We can rest today.
Let the dozy eye,
The one raised hip
Give no hint to the hours.

We are not done with toil:
Let rain work in these hours,
Wind in the night's hours,
We with the sun together
Tomorrow.

Midland, Ontario.

Full Moon

The moon is low...
The reddened face of a Chinese maiden
Aslant
Under light from Chinese lanterns,
A wisp of black fingers and wrist
Across its shame.

Towards midnight it rises
Still bent aslant
With a thick smile:
Until a slow line of blackness
Smothers it,
And only flung pink arms below
Are showing.

From a Train: Slums and Fields

I lounge in a chair and see
  The lives of men slip past
In dreams of all he would be,
  All have, that may not last.

Here, his passion brings forth
  Brothers' toil and loathing and wrath:
To show to himself the worth
  Of what he may move when he hath

– Himself not yet, not yet achieved –
  Only the breath of his steep-winged dream,
Only dearth and bitterness million-leaved
  Of yellow and rotting lives upon the stream.

Here, with passion exacting
  He stoops to the earth to find strife,
With the soil and himself compacting
  To make his Battle of Life.

And beyond the worth of that battle sees
  Again but himself in his need-filled fate.
If he rise and come on beauty in the lees,—
  Look, once, with distance-given eyes, it is too late.

    . . . . .

A corpuscle sped in a vein
  Of life, as I sit, am hurled
In the pulse of the speed of the train,
  I dream, cleaving a swift world.

23 December 1920. Blenheim, Ontario.

The Life in Letters

I: Awaiting the Bard

1

A young girl
Passing down the ways
Of the world
Looking, wistfully:
Is this He?
Could this be the man?
No, that one...
Perhaps this one?...

2

A worn-out woman
Awaiting her drunken lord,
Huddled at the fire
Starts —

Is that his step?...
But this, perhaps;
Or this...
If he come
Never?...

II: The Satirist

The oxen will not move.
The heavy-butted "black-snake" whip
Is in his fist:
But the nature of that black-snake?

Still, as he swings it
Its razored lash
Curls around his neck,
Tears his ears and his face.

The oxen do not budge;
They stand
And chew their cuds,
By times flick an ear backward
Appreciatively:
He will be finished presently,
Before he has learned.

They do not mind!

III: Critic and Author

He holds forth a mirror
(His own especial shaping)
Bent, convex, concave, or cannular.
The other will not look,
So he splinters it,
(Desperation)
On the averted head –
Effects
Anything but phantasmal!

IV: The Vivisectionist

He opens the heart
Of a bird of song.
He tightens the strings:
Queek!   Queek!
Hear them.
"Hear them!" he shouts,
Coming before the curtain,
To the mob, admiring,
"'Tis a bird;
Only better now,
He's singing now,
In a conscious impeccable way."

A Face in a Motor

I hailed you only with mine eyes,
   And though swiftly you were far away –
Before your smile had ceased to play –
   Still, unto the haven where Love lies
   I haled you with mine eyes.

I hailed you only with mine eyes,
   But I was sore appalled then –
I hoped that you felt lothly called then –
   By Fate's weird sneer, which for prize
   Haled you from before mine eyes.

4 February 1920.

On a Skyscraper

Dark comes
Smitten through
With white palsy of the storm.

Serried rank after rank
Unhurried wraith-legions
Wave past upon the roofs.

Below
In the canyoned street
Of blotted light
They whirl onward,
More purposed, ballasted more
Than the hungry
Swarming there
That they may feed
To toil more, to hunger
More, to feed
More
Winters.

January 1921. Blenheim, Ontario.

Dog and Cat

He sees my neighbour's cat
As sedately she walks in the garden.
He bounds toward her,
But she, certain of the fence,
Erects herself
And her fur,
Backing sidelong a little
With ear-laid hauteur:
I don't believe we've met before?

But he,
Remembering the fence now,
Merely wished to look through
At the flowers.
He does not look at her.
He scrubs the turf with his hind feet
Shooting forth grass-roots behind him,
Barks at a passing truck,
And comes home
Gallantly
Tail in air.

6 January 1921.

Minutiae

You sit on the grass
And you think old thoughts
Evanescent and misty and wide.
You speak to intent flowers.
You gesture with trees.

Your little dog awakes.
Pricks ears,
Rises, gallops gayley
As burlesquing a rocking horse
Stiffleggedly toward you.
Between two yelps
His cold nose meets
Your star-beckoning hand.

6 January 1921. Blenheim, Ontario.

Parting on the Beach

Tell me no more, love
   It was but a dreary dream...
The beach is wet, and high above
   The waves and the seagulls scream.

They tower aloud and bellow,
   As to bear us down if they might,
But their leapings hide not the mellow
   Gleam of love's starlight.

The stairs of the sea are keening,
   Fell the beat of my heart reply!
But why should your dream have meaning
   That I go out to die?

Tell me no more love
   'Twas but a foolish dream;
Think but to feebly none
   Avails, with the moving stream.

6 January 1921.

The poem was probably written about Keats, who tearfully left his wife before travelling to Italy where he died in the Spring of 1821, but is eerily prophetic of Knister's own death by drowning in 1932, witnessed by his wife on the beach of Lake St. Clair.

Ambition

When I was little,
And my father
And his men
Would mow back the hay
In the barn,
We liked to watch them,
To hang about
Playing, by times listening
To the talk of neighbours,
Of threshing-bees, of crops,
Of horses, every one by name,
And sheep and dogs,
And whether the storm would come
Before the last load.

But becoming tired of this,
One of us, Sid, it was, one day
Began to climb
Rung, by rung
The steep straight ladder
As high as the top
Of the load of hay.
Then he cried out:
"Look where I am!
To-om! Look where I am!"
Then Tom put out his little chin,
And began to climb,
His tongue upturned between his teeth.
Breathless, he mounted

To two rungs above Sid,
Who had hung there,
Watching him.
"I'm higher than you now, Sid!"
He shrilled, puffing
With pride and fear of falling.
"I'm higher'n you."
But now Sid began to climb again,
So Tom must too

Tom reached the beam
First, and sat down
On it, and looking across
Saw father's head
As he worked,
Up under the roof,
Rending apart the big bundles of hay,
And cried out,
"Papa! Look where I am!
I'm higher'n Sid!"
Then father, hearing his name,
Ceased his talking –
For he was used
To our uproar –
And said, "Get right down
Out o' there, get right down!
You'll fall and hurt yourselves!"
And I had just begun
To climb up the other ladder
At the far end of the driveway.

But what was I thinking of?...
Yes, Minnie, my wife,
And my daughters,
Since we've bought this estate,
How little they see, or wish
To see, of Tom's wife,
And Sid's
And their families... Except to...
Climbing.

Blenheim, Ontario.

Sumach

A little knoll
On the shoulder of the hill
Whisks the sumach bush
Under the nose of a cloud
Gaily.
He smiles
Pretends to sneeze
Playfully, –
Filling the valley with mist.

8 January 1921. Blenheim, Ontario.

The Roller

The trees still seem a reincarnation
Though the ground is dried and hard.
Hear, a mile away,
The tenor bellow of a roller
As it strikes the furrows.
The short corn will bend, to be sure,
But the soil will be flattened,
And rain on the broken lumps
Shall work an alchemy.

There is only the creak of harness
And the low words of teamsters
In the unplanted fields,
And in the field where the roller is
There shall be no more loudness
Until the wind rasps dried stalks
And boys shout to each other
Above the crisp surf-noise,
Among golden mounds of corn
Stretching in rows.

On "The Roller"

A roller is a very simple looking implement; it's a large metal cylinder, quite heavy, which horses used to and tractors still pull over cultivated ground in order to smooth out the lumps. "Tenor bellow of the roller" is exactly what it sounds like, and, for some reason or other, this suggests a great deal more than it seems to be saying. Is it that the simpler and more basic the activity, the closer we are to paradise? It's like that painting of the artist's old shoes: the intensity is multiplied by the humility of the subject.

– *James Reaney*. "Preface." *7.*

On "In The Rain, Sowing Oats"

A rich variety of sensual appeals creates a complex response, yet the poem remains simple, sharp and clear. The second section of the poem balances the image of a man against the image of the horses, and a subtle variation in tone emphasizes the differences between horses.

– *David Arnason*. "Canadian Poetry: The Interregnum." *31.*

In the Rain, Sowing Oats

The Horses

Cracked shoutings;
A heavy wet line swung down
To sting wet ribs,
Wet backs;
Aching jaws, aching necks
And blistered shoulders.

The Man

Shoes dragging the clods,
Eyes busy;
Arm-weight hanging limply
To the lines;
Thoughts of horses that take
Half the land for grain and hay;
Amid thoughts of supper.

Fall-time Milking

The air is silvered,
New grown clover glistens cold
Through and above the stubble.
Gus does not see.
While mist steams up from the jets and the pail,
Hangs pervasive and seen by part only,
Seeming the air's ghost made "isle"
He is thinking that two more days bring Sunday
And he can have the boss' horse and rig,
And two more months will bring
Card parties and dances
And he will see her
Three times a week.

Spring-flooded Ditches

Petulant, shading her stare,
The moon
Looks a second
(Fearing all things
Are unchanged)
At Clym Norton's bridge
Which hangs
On the lift of the floodike ditch.

Raymond Knister

Long-rolling splash of the buggy
Down clay ruts,
Neat quiet clipping
Of fluttered telephone-pole shadows –
Wind upon the wires,
Wash of the ditch
About the necks of last year's
Weeds:
To whom
Music is strange
Your music is Strange :
A farmhand's past.

See alternate version.

White Cat

I like to go to the stable after supper, –
Remembering fried potatoes and tarts of snow-apple jam –
And watch the men curry the horses,
And feed the pigs, and especially give the butting calves their milk.
When my father has finished milking he will say,
"Now Howard, you'll have to help me carry in these pails.
How will your mother be getting along
All this time without her little man?"
So we go in, and he carries them, but I help.
My father and I don't need the lanterns.
They hang on the wires up high back of the stalls
And we leave them for Ern and Dick.
It seems such a long way to the house in the dark,
But sometimes we talk, and always
There's the White Cat, that has been watching
While my father milked.
In the dark its gallop goes before like air,
Without any noise,
And it thinks we're awfully slow
Coming with the milk.

On "The White Cat"

The poem "White Cat" illustrates how Knister's poetry can blend attention to different but continuous aspects of reality. Simplicity marks the poem's opening line.... The second line... belies the simplicity of the opening line by evoking memory, sensory perception, and highly specific, and local, detail. The boy who is the narrator of the poem refers to a "White Cat" that crosses his path as he and his father return, "with the milk," from the stable to the house. Knister leaves precisely what the "White Cat" stands for open to question. The White Cat may be an ordinary pet seen with the intensity of unfettered or unjaded imagination, be a figment of the boy's active imagination, symbolize imagination itself, or even represent a combination of possible meanings. In Knister's poem, whatever the White Cat itself may mean, there is a discoverable excitement to everyday life. The power of the boy's imagination enables him to perceive magic in the so-called ordinary. Knister suggests that the magic stems from everyday life — it is not antithetical to it.

– *Joy Kuropatwa*. Raymond Knister and His Works. *16.*

The Motor: A Fragment

Joyous as azure sky,
Uncabined as the beauty of greenery,
Onward –
Ten joyous miles ahead.

In flashing sequence I see my brothers
Draw down toward me as by a magnet pulled,
And I to them;
Sharks in coral sea bearing down upon the prey,
Progress an endless tourney
And cleaving of whirled comet-tails.

Down, down the slope,
To flow in effortless speed,
To brake, to slacken,
Leashed power that gives me joy.

Past the fields of clover
In the sunlight crisping,
And the fence-posts spryly jumping toward me,
Over streams that shiver and dance,
Clefts and ravines to echo
At my rush over the wooden bridges
With their rattling planks.

Past the huge wheat-fields
Dry-smelling and toasting.
Up the long hill in a burst
Of splendid speed,
Unleashed power, that gives me joy.

To swoop like a bird over crossings
And the rises at the heads of farmer's lanes,
Past farm-houses deeply over-woven:
Trees, vines, gardens and flowers;
Past the dismal unshaded farm-houses,
Keys to parched lives.
Past farms quiet and busy and sane, with weedy fronts,
Past homes of the idler, and the man who would kill himself
With the pride of his work,
That have no weeds along the road.

Oh for the swift ride at night –
Mile after joyous mile,
Swift, and with splendid unleashed power
That gives me joy...
A rut, a twist of the wheels,
Swaying speed,
And the pale terrible face of danger
Just glimpsed, only the fairy grace of it seen...
Throb and purr
Mile on joyous mile.

An Old Wooden Windmill

Mornings it used to stand proudly,
Vane a white arm out-thrown derisively to the chasing breeze.
Long wings twirled with languid and throbbing swiftness.

Afternoons
It peeked across pasture-land and bush-land, between the trees,
Burnished silver until sun-down.

Came nights of infuriate storm,
Years in the nights,
Frenzied whirlings through the long dark:
The rag-wheel broken.

Now,
No mercy from caprice of cloud
Of any whipping breeze to twitch the leaves.
Its own is the wind's wild will.
Dark and gaunt-framed,
Blue and veering in the day,
In the night
With rusty, sudden,
Loud complainings
It 'frights the birds, asleep.

Blenheim, Ontario. See alternate version.

East Side

Joachim Moujiski is at home tonight. All day at the docks
     his feet and his hands have been strong. Now, his
     grey heavy shoes are in the corner, and his hand
     with yellow callouses holds Kusimhoff's book,
     "Regimes of Evil", lent him by a so-wise friend.
     Last night Joachim was with a Federation meeting.
     Tomorrow night he will be with a Federation meeting.

Joachim is going to understand, to learn about things.
     About all things in time, about these things first.
     Now he sits unmoving in the rocking-chair. His dark socks
     splotch the dull oil-cloth. Kusimoff's book
     is unopened.

For his sister sits at the old black piano. Her notes
     are spattering raindrops from high boughs in spring
     on shaded violets in forest depths.

                    They blend
                    to the turbid roar
                    of a sad unminding river
                    in the dark
                    in the still night
                    after storm,
                    away to unseen banks,
                    away to undreamed seas

Joachim has an old thought that troubles and troubles in
    sweet persistence, unseizable. His eyes do not see.
    This thing he does not understand, and only afterwards
    can wonder at.

Bees

Snow-drops hang
Dancing,
Lifting and flitting
Tiny
Through the swarm,
Never striking;
Hum about the tamarack,
Drift a little
Toward the cabin window:
Too late.
The honey of frost-flowers is melted –
Too late.

Blenheim, Ontario.

The Ploughman

All day I follow
Watching the swift dark furrow
That curls away before me,
And care not for skies or upturned flowers,
And at the end of the field
Look backward
Ever with discontent.
A stone, a root, a strayed thought
Has warped the line of that furrow –
And urge my horses 'round again.

Sometimes even before the row is finished
I must look backward;
To find, when I come to the end
That there I swerved.

Unappeased I leave the field,
Expectant, return.

The horses are very patient.
When I tell myself
This time
The ultimate unflawed turning
Is before my share,
They must give up their rest.

Blenheim, Ontario. See alternate version.

On "The Poughman"

His concern with the undeviatingly linear, his strict attention to his work, differentiates him from the ploughman in "Ploughman's Song" [see page 124] who is associated with a recognition of curvilinearity, who does not allow his consciousness to be chained to the patterns of his work, and whose song acknowledges the continuity between the worlds of man and nature.

— *Joy Kuropatwa*. Raymond Knister and His Works. *20.*

On "Poisons"

"Poisons" is as modern in its concern as it is in its prose-poem form. It describes in rich and rhythmic prose, the spraying of peach trees.... The spraying machine in seen in animal terms, as a sort of prehistoric monster, its breath the poison spread to the pink blossoms. The ecological concern is particularly modern.

— *David Arnason*. "Canadian Poetry: The Interregnum." *32.*

Poisons

Slow down the peach-rows drives Gil Alberts. He sits
    high on the weighty spray outfit, weighty with a
    heaviness alive, as it lurches and rolls through
    soft wet gravel to sniffle and spit for its firing
    engine and dogged groan and whine of pumps.

At each young tree he stops a moment, moving on slowly
    at once.

(The bay horses are long-haired and soft from the winter.
    Their two heaved breaths at each stopping rocks the
    Machine a little. At each shout of Gil as the tree's
    finished they pull in their heads and stamp onward,
    sweat about the roots of their ears, hearing the
    relentless bark and swift whine of engine and pump.)

Beside him is a yellow trumpet of fog from the gun, two
    hundred pounds pressure of poison loosened on the
    pink well-rooted young trees.

He thinks of a yellow green poison-cloud four years, four
    thousand miles away, the sight through gas masks,
    through slit of the swivelled gun, in the roar and the
    rhythm unabolished by lurchings, as the tank gropes
    forward.

At one side of him, now, wide strips of yellow green lie wet
    on the gravel and dried grass of last summer along the
    tree rows.

As he turns at the long orchards and the sun makes a rain-
     bow halo of yellow-green poison.

Never forgetting, Gil Alberts keeps his well-timed pull of
     the reins, his well-timed shout to the horses at the
     calls of his brother as each tree's done. Rolling
     amid the bark and sniffle and whine of engine and
     pump they pass down another row, about them the hiss
     of poison to pink young trees.

October Stars

Was it the frenzied whisper
Of covert wind to obdurate apple-boughs,
(Leaves sheltering no more fruit)
Or the paled sky drawing in,
Or the peal of a shooting-star
Across the night?
Or did all these
And the tame apple-smell
Through the wind in your hair
Make me to long
For an end to life?

Blenheim, Ontario.

Raymond Knister

The Hawk

Across the bristled and sallow fields,
The speckled stubble of cut clover,
Wades your shadow.

Or against a grimy and tattered
Sky
You plunge.

Or you shear a swath
From trembling tiny forests
With the steel of your wings –

Or make a row of waves
By the heat of your flight
Along the soundless horizon.

On "The Hawk"

"The Hawk" employs the technique of Imagism, but is more interesting in content than Imagist poems ordinarily are. Knister had his own distinguishing qualities. He had learned – almost alone among Canadian writers of the twenties – the principle requisite of free verse: that cadence and feeling must be thoroughly fused.

– *Munro Beattie.* "Poetry 1920-1935." *729.*

As descriptive poetry, this can stand with anything written by any poet in the twentieth century, whatever his country. The poem is at once incisively clear, and brilliantly evocative.

– *David Arnason.* "Canadian Poetry: The Interregnum." *32.*

Possession

What shall I call your spell,
  Moonlight on rippling trees,
Dew on blanched lilacs in a dell?
  But things like these

Are too cold, too tranced and pale
  And at their nearest, far,
To speak of you or to avail;
  For though you are

A light to the eye in darkness, keep
  Strange with the music known
Of unseen waves in valleys deep,
  You're just "My Own"!

Snowfall

Floating and sifting
Into earth's eyes,
Dimming their wildness.

Into her ears
Sifting and floating,
Numbing the discords.

Muffling the thrum
Of pulses, the fever
With pale bright sleep.

Sifting and floating...

Blenheim, Ontario. See alternate versions.

On "Snowfall"

With a sigh, I hie, to "Snowfall." You request that the 2nd line read "Into earth's eyes." Very well. You request that the omission of lines 4 & 8. What I mean by line 4 (Do not all poets suspect others of not understanding them? I hope, at any rate that I'm not lonely in that attribute) is that the melting snow particles in her eyes cause her to see the spectrum colours. For the 8th line, even I can find no justification except that, like the articles of attire of one of O'Henry's characters, it "balances perfectly" with line 4.

> – *Raymond Knister. Letter to Louise Nicholl (editor of* The Measure*). 1.8.1921.*

I was so glad that you liked "Snowfall." Slight as it is, I think it is about as good as anything I've done... These people who are agin free verse can't have read any farther back than Ella Wheeler Wilcox.

> – *Raymond Knister. Letter to John T. Frederick (editor of* The Midland*). 21.11.1921.*

Corn Husking

I

"Hold still now! Hold still, say! you can't slip it –"

The horse finishes her grain at a gulp, and I add,
"You want your bonnet on right, old girl,
For I don't want to quit my husking just
To put it on again, you bet, and get away behind
The other fellows on my row – Go on!
Jake's standing down there, and's had his drink.
Move 'long!"

II

While I've been harnessing the horses up
The other boys have been pitching off
The morning's last load of corn. The big
Barrack walled up two-plank-high
Is empty now, and they both wait
While I bring up the team. Jess won't drink.
"Come, you've not signed a pledge?" And I knock
Each heel to other. "Well, come on." Four of us
Dodge about the horses, fore and rear,
Snapping lines, tossing them to the box,
Lifting the tongue, shouting the two forward
To fasten the neck-yoke, shouting the "Back!"
To hook the traces up. "First link them, boy,
You're forgetting!" Four of us for Father
Has come forth from the pig-pen. "All aboard!"

he shouts, and the three of us clamber up
While he stays behind to shut the lane gate.
Then he's on; I loosen up the lines
And slap the horses on, and everybody reels
Turning the corner. The wind brushes our ears,
We shout, sing, dance a ballet to the sober cloud gradings,
And the cornstalks bow with laughter. Quickly
We jump from the wagon. The horses promptly
Seize stalks, snorting. (The corn's husked here
Or it's ears they'd grab.) I fix the lines to the board,
And the corn thumps and splinters about me
And when I'm down, my row is left behind.

III

For a time I'm busy tearing out the corn.
(Whoever is ahead gives the horses the word,
"Git up!" "Come along here!" or "Move along,
Boys and girls". And when you've got behind
You don't like to hear those words.) The rustling,
Quick and crackling, and the staccato pounding
Of the corn upon the floor fills my mind
For a time, as I struggle forward, and my movement
Struggles toward a rhythm. Then I begin to hear
My father talking, and in a minute, of course,
Am able to catch up again. He is pretending
To tease our Bill. "Well, Roy, I'm getting tired
Of bacon all the time, I'd like to have
A whack at a good fat duck, you bet."

And Bill replies, "My old man's gone ducking
At the Marsh", as though he hadn't said the same
Two or three times before that day.
"What's that?
Roy, just you wait 'till Bill's old man gets home,
He'll give me one, and two to you, and just
Save four for himself Then when mine's all gone,
I'll just go down and call on Bill some night
At suppertime, and won't we have a feed!
Gid up; come on here, boys and girls – Yes sir."
Roy then takes up the cue, and when the wagon stops
He winks at me, and says, while Bill works on
With soberness assumed as the best thing
Under the circumstances, not to take
The invitation as a joke, "Oh, your
Dad's gone to the Marsh, is he, Bill? And what
Is he going to do with all the ducks?"
"Oh, he will only have a few, maybe."

"What if he has a couple of dozen, or so?"

"Oh, he'll give three to me and five to you,
And all the rest he'll have for himself.."
"Never mind, Billy! – Get up here, Jess! Jake! –
You'll have to take some over to the Irish Line
At any rate. – Don't blush! – I hear that you
Go over there every night to see, –
Who is it now?
"Sam Grady's daughter, eh?"

From Roy, "Or maybe Tim O'Shea's; he'll give
Bill one of his big farms when he gets through."
This switches Father. "Say, have you seen how
The corn is on that back place, you know which,
The one he was going to sell; is't good?"
Roy and my father then rehearse the whole
Of what came near a sale, and yet was not
Because old Tim "backed out" when came the time;
In an evocative way, one will tell
One fact of it, as though the other had
Never heard of the farm, nor guessed of what
Had taken place. Then the other takes up
The theme, and tells his version of a part.
When they have finished it at last with help
Thrown in from me, a smile still holds its place
On Bill's red face; "You've not guessed right at all"
Says he, or murmurs to the crashing stalks.
My row is nearest his, and he is left
Behind just then, so I am helping him.
"Big job it is; To make a choice, eh Bill?"

"I chose one long ago," he says and grins.

IV

On we go, down the half-mile rows.
Less talking now, because the end is near.
The air is cool, the wind is sharp, not strong
But buoyant. Wisps of long torn leaves of corn
Are floating high like tiny barges, tarnished gold,
Until, after a minute's cruise at most,

They slide prow-first into the deep, and spill
Their load invisible. And all about
The tones of sepia, old gold, dirt-brown,
Ink-blue in forests farther off; a sky
All dusty, and not cleansed yet with the snow.
The ground is blackened deep with recent wet.
Bill wears his rubber boots, which are too big,
And make his thin legs seem bowing
Different angles as he walks. As we go on
Roy tosses an ear toward the wagon carelessly,
And it goes down inside Bill's boot. Roy laughs.
Bill says, "Here, take this corn, I don't want what
Is not my own."
"Wait a bit, Roy", says Father,
"We'll not fill Bill's boots until the wagon won't
Hold any more. Then a few bushels, eh,
If Bill doesn't object? But not until
The wagon has all it will hold."

"Well, why do you keep wearing those blamed boots
When it is getting dry again? Unhealthy, boy." –
It has been a silent joke to Roy the few days past.
"They're good; you don't get wet in these," says Bill,
And mutters more, convincing only to himself,
Amid the rattle of the stalks of corn
Upon the wagon, "Here's the end at last!"
And Bill and I begin to rush, for fear,
(We happen to be the last, although we've been
Ahead more than once coming down the rows)
For fear of being helped by the others.
Instead of that, my father makes a jump

And pulls the ears in 'round the edge,
Gathers up his lines, and waits 'til we come.

He stops the horses once or twice to give
Them breath. (The ground is soft and loose.)
While we will use the time to pull
The husks that still hold, stubborn to the corn.

V

At first we all get on our knees,
Two at each end, and throw the corn
In handfuls from the load, but when a hole
Is made so we can use our shovels
Then Roy and I seize hold of them, and send
My father up to fetch us apples back
And pull straw out to bed the stock for the night.
Oh man, perhaps those shovels do not sing
As each ear-cluster shoots from the metal,
For we are getting chilled from the long ride,
And as the metal sings the kernels dance,
Their golden drops sparkling as they leap up,
Knocked from the hard ear-parents as they strike.
A golden popping like one hears merely,
In popcorn pans, is seen around each shovelful,
And watching we forget the flight of time
Until we see the load is nearly off,
And Bill, throwing from the middle, must leave
The rest to us. Then Father comes, we pull
Our jackets on, munch apples and drive out.
"Hold on there!" Father cries, "You have forgot

To pick the corn up that is on the floor."
Then we jump off and throw it up, to give
Next load a clear headway.

VI

At first the row too long stretches before us.
A little while we're slow and lax
Of motion. But soon we have gained headway
Again, and soon are trying speeds. There is
A rainy pounding on the wagon's floor.
"You'd think 'twas raining corn," says Bill, and jerks
His ear loose. Every move is rhythmic now;
Left hands grip ears, swing wrist, and throw
Aloft toward the box. Once I catch Bill
In stride, right leg flung forth, right arm outstretched
As he tosses forth an ear and makes for the next stalk...
Small time I have to watch what others do,
But keep wielding my peg as best I may.
But I can see the air is full of husks
On ears, a white snowstorm with flakes as huge
As oak leaves in the fall. "Now boys, now boys;"
We hear, "We've got to husk 'em cleaner'n this."
Just then a red ear falls upon the load,
"That's mine," says Bill.
"Yours, eh," my father says,
"That's nice. You know the old French custom?"
"No, what is it?"
"You *don't*? Now that is strange.
A young fellow like you I'd think would know
These things right off by heart. Well, when they're husking

In the field (the young girls husk too, you know)
And anyone, young girl or man, throws out
An ear that's red, like that one is,
He or she may take their choice, to kiss
Whichever one is at the bee, they like."

"Oh that's it, eh?" young Bill replies
With a little chin-jerking laugh.
A vision comes of those young humans years ago,
Boys in home-tailoring, caps
Of black, and girls with petticoats, and shawls
About their heads, as we move on. The corn
Is bent over with the wind in some places,
And we must stoop quite low to seize each ear.
Hard on the back it is, a little bit.
Then Roy begins to hum, and whistle soft,
"The last Rose of Summer".
"Give me the last
Rows of corn", Bill says, "and you can have
The rose of summer."

VII

The early dusk is coming on, gathered in
The long pale rows of bowing corn, and from
The sky, and from the thick dark trees far off
About the country's edge, it seems to come.
Slowly it gathers in about us where we work.
The sun is going too, south-west of us,
And does not seem to want to light things up a bit
Just for a farewell shot, as he will sometimes do.

"It only seems a little while," says Bill
"Since that old sun used to go down away
To the north-west, but now, the rate he's going
He'll soon be setting in the south, it looks".
There is no answer, no one thinks of it,
We just keep stooping, jerking out the ears.
My father moves along, bent all the time,
Never straightening up. The sun goes down
With defiant splendour, as though he cares
Nothing for all the disregarding men
On the flat land, bent to the soil behind
Their ploughs, or husking corn, or hauling stalks,
Or in long rail-fenced lanes, driving cattle home.
"Soon we'll have to feel for them", for Bill
Is always anxious when night comes on
Or noon, for that matter; time cannot be
Urged on enough to suit him then.
But he looks up, and sees a long and sinuous V
Wavering toward us. Wild geese flying
Toward the south above our heads. We stop
Our rustling in the husks and look, all still
Except the horses plucking at the stalks –
"Just wish I had my gun," says Bill. "Oh boy!"

"You'd never reach those birds from here, oh boy."
"Oh yes I would, they're not so high!"
"Listen," I say, for there comes down a squeak,
A mellowed squeak, like a pitiful baby-cry
One and another of the great birds gives
As they cleave space, and, almost, time, across the night.

"Why, they're encouraging each other on".
Says Father, then, "Well boys, we've got to move
Along ourselves. Jess! Jake! Get up, get up!"
The ears are really getting hard to see.
"How many miles does this row go, you know?"
"Ends opposite that tree along the fence",
Says Roy.
"That big one over there, you mean?...
It looks as if it had no end at all.
You can't tell when you're opposite that tree,
It may be fifty yards we've got to go."
But it's nearer five, we find.
We lie upon the solid corn and pluck
Idly at wisps of husks, and see we have
Forgotten to take off the pegs. Then each
Recites how his hands are scarred and raw;
And Father tries to stop the team, but they
Will only rest a breath, then jerk ahead.
"They know when's suppertime," young Bill remarks.

"Well I can smell supper on the stove
From here," says Roy. We all agree to that.
Rhythmically the bent stalks click and brush
Against the axle as the wagon moves.

On "Corn Husking"

While "Corn Husking" is atypical of Knister's work in being a longer poem, it includes a number of elements that recur in his poetry. The poem covers a day of working at corn husking, as seen from the point of view of the son of the farmer who leads the harvest. "Corn Husking" illustrates the sharpness of Knister's eye for the details that conjure up a particular environment. In giving fragments of good-humoured teasing and gossip, as well as sights nad sounds of the working environment, Knister conveys why it is the work does not become grindingly monotonous.

– *Joy Kuropatwa*. Raymond Knister and His Works. *29*.

Windfalls for Cider [1925]

[It] is not likely that we will reach indigenous Canadian forms at the first try, so that experiment has always seemed perilous. It will perhaps need many generations of farm boys who find a soul in the pigs they are feeding and romance in their furrows, before we produce that perfect singing voice of a Shropshire lad. It is from this sense that I would call my book Windfalls for Cider. Many Chattertons may come before a Burns. Burnses do not spring from the void; but undoubtedly this country will yet produce a great poet from its soil.

– Raymond Knister, in a letter to Lorne Pierce, 23.11.1925.

Poems selected, and introduced, by Raymond Knister for a book that was not published during his lifetime.

Foreword: Windfalls for Cider

Men and women write poems because they are moved by things.

It is a fine thing to be moved, fine to know that what you write will move others. Because it is so, people are in a hurry to write poems. They look for subjects, perhaps they read a lot. There are plenty of subjects. They write.
If people did not know poetry should be written, they would be moved none the less. Perhaps not so often, nor by the same things. They might feel that some truck-driver had a finer face than Gallahad; or that two men in broiling sun pitching dry clover that fell in chaff upon their sweaty heads were more impressive than neatly draped statues to Labour. What are they going to do about it? That is not poetry, it is life. Life is likely to be troublesome as times. Let us veil it, they say, in sonorous phrases and talk about birds and flowers and dreams.

Birds and flowers and dreams are real as sweating men and swilling pigs. But the feeling about them is not always so real, any more, when it gets into words. It has been derived. Because of that, it would be good just to place them before the reader, just let the reader picture them with the utmost economy and clearness, and let them be moved in the measure that he is moved by little things and great. Let him snivel, or be uncaring, or make his own poems from glimpsed undeniable images of the world.

It would be good for the flowers and birds and dreams, and good for us. We would love them better, and be more respectful. And we might feel differently about many other things if we saw them clearly enough. In the end, we in Canada here might have the courage of our experience and speak according to it only, And when we trust surely, see directly enough life, ourselves, we may have our own Falstaffs and Shropshire Lads and Anna Kareninas.

We may climb ladders, and our apples will be hand-picked, and make a more lasting vintage.

Raymond Knister, Toronto, 1 December 1926.

After Exile

Waking...
This train spreads land
After a gloom of intents teeming
Turmoil of lost
Streets,
A world
After chaos.

There is the sky
Wants to know nothing,
Here pulling the wheels is earth
That yet can wait.

Sorrow can be sweet at last.

Factories to weed-land:
Then:
Roads, tawny, clot
In farmyards, packed clay stares,
(The time is even October.)
But barns, houses are fettered.

Youth whirls the dust.
Old men cast horse-shoes
Cast by old horses.
Across pastures, through a surf of golden-rod
Boys wade; Sunday,
And there may be mushrooms.

The corn like drunken grenadiers
Topples tarnished
Whispering
At the hooting train.

Grapevines know that which they hide.
Houses, pig-sties clustered,
Church and church-shed,
Weigh-scales,
General wires crossed
Whirl.
(It is not at no cost I see it all,
See a simple and quaint pattern
Like the water-mark in this paper,
There if you like, or if you forget,
Not there.
It is the same.)

It is the same,
The pathos of bitter living
Irrelevant like the memory of a wrong you would for-
give if it had hurt you.

The same crows, susurrant,
Wake the shrill bush
All day.

At nightfall, in the smeared haze
The boy stumbles over pumpkins
And finds earth itself
Feigning death.

And is it the apples they have piled
Or the sudden dark of trees,
Stripped writhing of quince-trees,
Fatal stoic sanguine red-oak, –
Did they all tell the men in the wind,
Death
Bids you satisfy yourself
With food, drink and slumber?

      (This train is the clicked passing of
      Dreams,
      Never tires disposing...
      The swing of telegraph wires
      A cradle to sense.

      The couple across the aisle don't know whether to
          smile at frank words and contortions
          of their babies,
          or toss heads at one a stranger who in an hour
          will not exist ...)

The tattoo, tattoo of fingers on dinner-pails
As the boys come home from school,
Of wild knees on mangers
When the weary hired man
Raises his fork behind the colts.

Roads will be white again
And sleighs bear white loads,
Dressed pork from yesterday's

Raucous killing:
"Are you sure the mares are not in foal?"
They snort and sleigh-runners squeal.

The thinned trees
Cleave the snow-light.
Echoes sound
And follow
Taunting
The logs rolled up, chained,
And asleep on the silent sleigh.

The horses have forgotten the ford,
They cross the snow-covered ice
With no pause of the jingling bells.
"This'll hold that old furnace, make us some biscuits."
The yard is full of sawings and splittings.

Snow,
Boys,
Dogs,
Rabbits fly,
The sun...

But before they know it, the black land steams
And crusts with frost, and steams.
Oats fields are ready.
Horses nodding breast the sharp air,
The sun spreads.
Man follows and forgets all once more
But to watch the ground passing under.

It is the same.

That he loves, or has forgotten
Is a weariness
Of half-sought memory.
Until, another harvest come,
Gone,
He may remember that this is life
And think to be wise
Seeing it pass.

On "After Exile"

He returned to Canada in October, 1924. His journey homeward became the source of one of his finest poems, "After Exile." He meant this poem "to synthesize one individual reaction to the environment that represents his country" [Letter to Florence Livesay 15.9.1925]. "After Exile" describes a train moving slowly through the spreading land and unravels a ribbon of images which tells the story of the land's ongoing harvest. As these images are braided into the consciousness of the poet-observer, they are coloured by memories of his past life…. As "After Exile" suggests, Knister's consciousness was awakening to his old, yet new, environment. He approached it with a confident, newly matured energy.

> – *Marcus Waddington.* "Raymond Knister: A Biographical Note." *181.*

Sea-Blue Eyes

When I looked into the sorrow
Of your sea-blue eyes
It was a world, my glimpse
Of faerie
The mist concealed;
And I waited for the sun.

But though the strange imagined
Wonders were not there,
The blue is as endless
In the dancing light.

Blenheim, Ontario

Haunted House

Is it the trill of crickets
In the weeds
CLEEK – CLEEK …
Or the pulsing in the brain
Of the ghost,
The ghost of that woman
Maddened here at these brightened windows
By the same clouded August moon –
Buried, as then,
In the smell of these weeds?

Reply to August

What is the word that night is saying,
Dark night, still?
The curtains waver, but the unheard voice
Makes no pause at the sill.

The room does not know it has heard
But I know,
My heart listening, wild with the word
Murmured too low.

I shall hear what the nights have told, –
Another night
When this heart is the word it is speaking
In clouds' hush or starlight...

Northwood, Ontario.

On "A Row of Stalls"

A dozen free verse poems about horses which I had published in *This Quarter* of Paris, might give you a better notion of my capabilities. The language could not be plainer, nor the material more homely. Yet a definite impression is made in each case, I think, along with some sense of the life which produced them. The art which conceals art seems to me best... The exclusively rural subject matter should not deceive you – my next book will be about life in Chicago.

– Raymond Knister. Letter to Olaf P. Rechnitzer. 09.04.1930.

A Row of Stalls

Lily

In the buggy
She can trot
Faster than a woman talks.
Here on the heavy wagonload
With old Nell, twice her weight
She needs the doubletree set over.
At the barn grade she digs in,
Upholds her end,
And her ears and nodding coquettish head
Tells her pride in tripping feet
That hold the big load
Beside this vast mate.

Nell

Nellie Rakerfield
Came from an estate in Scotland,
Two years old and won a championship.
It was not her fault that her foals
Were few, and mostly died or were runted.
She worked every day when she raised them,
Never was tired of dragging her
Nineteen hundred pounds
About the farm and the roads, with
Great loads behind it.
She never kicked, bit, nor crowded
In the stall,

Was always ready at a chirp
And seemed to have forgotten delicate care.

But the day they hitched her
To the corpse of her six-months-old colt,
She tried to run away, half way to the bush.
She never seemed quite so willing, afterward.
But the colt was too heavy.

See alternate version.

Mack

"Circus 'oss," the English hired man called him
Because he caught his old splay foot
In the harness when he tried to reach
A green fly,
And went twirling
Round and round, at the water trough.

He wouldn't drink with a bridle on,
And it was as hard to get the bridle off as on him,
For he would use his head like a club.
When he was young one master beat him on the ears,
And made him a little crazy.
As he walks he will nip at his mate, with fierce eyes
And a Roosevelt-Wilson-Fairbanks smile.
When he is asked to trot, he will jerk the unwary driver
And set up a gallop.
His rump, the shape of an upturned skiff,
Seems to rock on waves of dusty air.

Princess

Daughter of Nell,
She is proud as though she knew
Her length of pedigree.
She is keen and fleet as a race-horse,
And will wheel dangerously
At colts and elderly pasture horses;
But blood tells: she won't kick them,
Except Lily.
When Princess, four years old,
Full grown in pastures and box stalls,
Ready to be broken,
Was led into the stable past Lily,
The little blood mare squealed and bit the manger;
And it was never safe to let them out together.
They knew that they were the finest creatures
On the place.

Dinah

"Tough as seven-year-old lightning",
Rusted black in colour,
With a dash of Thoroughbred blood,
She lurked back and let the others
Do the work,
In the field.
And even in the buggy-shafts she would catch the line
With her tail, and kick desperately until it was released.

But with a saddle and rider
She found herself, and liked to race Fords.
As she galloped she heard one,
And her hoof-beats became swifter
Like raindrops of a downpour.
But that's not five times a year.
Perhaps in another life she will be favoured more,
And will be a Sappho or Bernhardt.

Cross-bred Colt

It gets its way
Among the bigger colts
Without kicking or biting,
By sheer fierceness of expression,
Seeming to know that it has no name,
And that nobody will care,
Until it is big enough to work.

The only time its ears were not flattened back
Was when the hired boy, tired
Of its regularly striking and tipping the waterpail
When the others crowded it,
Swung a clip to its muzzle.
It turned away and stood awhile,
Ears pricked,
Considering – the first contact with man –
Or was it pure surprise?

Baron Balderston

From the high window of his narrow box stall
He could see the sunshine,
The colts wheeling in the lane,
Old Nell his dam on the three-horse disc-harrow,
But he never got out.

Yet when he was small he had bran soaked in milk,
And constant cleanings,
Freedom with the other colts;
And when, five years old,
Of mountainous vastness,
He was sold to a horseman,
He passed over vast spaces of country
Attended and coddled by a brace of English valets,
Among his peers
In many thronged fairs.

Sam

Sam was just horse.
Nothing happened to him
Except long furrows,
Pasture-romps,
And long days in the stall.

Yet, one night
Lord Lochinvar, sire of Baron Balderston,
Whom a rival horseman poisoned later,
Broke out of the box-stall

And tore his neck with clamping teeth.
The owner heard Sam's scream,
But he always carried the mark.

Nance

"She kicked her foot throught the dashboard,
And I made her go, for about a mile."
The old cattle-dealer's booming voice,
Like that,
Must have lent speed to her three legs.
Then when they got home
He carefully unharnessed her,
Clutched her bridle in one hand,
Half a rail in the other,
And the dance began.

When Art Huffer got Nance,
He declared that he would cure her.
He took ten bushels of corncobs
Into the loft above her stall;
All the rainy day he dropped cobs
And as each one struck her
She kicked as high as ever:
Art had to give up too.

Lide

She was the team-mate of Nell,
Older, nearly as big, and snappy,
In action, always wanting to be ahead,

So that a green driver might kill her.
But her pedigree was not that of Nellie Rakerfield's.

So her colts were allowed to run wild,
And one died before a veterinarian was got.
She became old quickly,
And clover-poisoning made ugly
Her large white face with its small nostrils,
Her white-haired legs.
She passed, sold, from hand to hand.

Cliff

He stayed alone in a box-stall
Bedded with shavings from the planing mill,
Hearing the rattle of the mill
And the streets, alone
Months,
Until he was hitched in the buggy
To go down country roads, collecting.
One trip took him to the mill-man's brother-in-law;
There he was left
To be of some use.

The first time he was let out in the barnyard
With the other horses,
He didn't know what to do.
He wouldn't let them near him, kicked:
Even ran after them to corner them and kick
Desperately.
"Why he's a Tartar, would've crippled them, wicked."

The farmer wouldn't turn Cliff out again
Until by and by he became used to the others,
Was not afraid,
But quite peaceable.

Maud and Jess

After special care, rapid growth,
They were sold for trucking in the city.
Hard pavements, bad shoeing, corns, burnings,
Made them old.
They came to the farm together
And knew soft soil and rollings under pasture trees
Again.

Other horses, lighter, quick,
Might try to bully or tease,
But they always kept their solid black forms
Together,
And bothered none.
Presently their own colts took the place
Of these others.

Wind's Way

I shall sing with the whoop of the wind
When the strong wind comes plying,
And tall corn twists and clover shakes
And white-leaved trees are crying.

For the way of the wind with city smoke
– Its dark care spun into sky –
With white, bent sails on a rising bay,
And rapturous swallows shot by,

For its way with field-scent, voices, road-dust,
Girl's hair on my cheek to sting,
With manes of running pasture horses:
For wind's way with my heart I'll sing.

Port Dover, Ontario

Boy Remembers in the Field

What if the sun comes out
And the new furrows do not look smeared?

This is April, and the sumach candles
Have guttered long ago.
The crows in the twisted apple limbs
Are as moveless and dark.

Drops on the wires, cold cheeks,
The mist, the long snorts, silence...
The horses will steam when the sun comes;
Crows go, shrieking.

Another bird now; sweet...
Pitiful life, useless,
Innocently creeping
On a useless planet
Again.

If any voice called, I would hear?
It has been the same before.
Soil glistens, the furrow rolls, sleet shifts, brightens.

Dilettante

She will not write to me, and so
I cannot forget.
Her silence, more than pledges
Binds me in a net.

The wistful smiling memories
Are not for me,
The promised unfulfillment
Is bitter luxury.

Consummation

I hear a frenzied windmill whirling in the dusk.
I see the wind's grey steed of doom.
I smell the blown-down apples like a musk.
I taste the black hail-bitten loam.
And touch proud Death within a "living room".

Northwood, Ontario.

Speculation in a Flower Market

Is it so much, when one is old,
To know the buds one would not buy
Not worth the hoarding of this gold
– For fires to picture flowers by?

See alternate version.

Autumn Clouds

Here on the quiet upland
Among the withered corn
Wondering I stand:
Beauty again is born.

The thin light melts and yields,
The torn stalks shiver;
On near and far-off fields
I see pale gold, a river

That floats the fences, trees,
Golden-rod, and tarnished grasses,
A lift of brown like bees,
Submerges all, and passes

Leaving all no less unspent,
Nor more lonely. And I find,
Long lost, the trees' assent
To sunlight and to wind.

Blenheim, Ontario.

Quiet Snow

The quiet snow
Will splotch
Each in the row of cedars
With a fine
And patient hand;
Numb the harshness,
Tangle of that swamp.
It does not say,
The sun
Does these things another way.

Even on hats of walkers,
The air of noise
And street-car ledges
It does not know
There should be hurry

Northwood, Ontario.

Immemorial Plea

There is night and the rain-filled air
  With thunder far away,
And tremor of lightning shows all fair
  The earth beneath its play.

What else could I crave, as I sit here
   And hearken all the lore
Of leaves, as each leaf sings its joy in fear –
   Save only you, what more?

Each leaf is rapture in all the tree,
   And you too should be kind;
And after, rise and go through lanes with me,
   Rain-bitten dust, sad wind.

Port Dover, Ontario

Moments When I'm Feeling Poems

Moments when I'm feeling poems –
Before the stir and clash of words –
When some forgotten clear slight
Secret's imminent plangent chords

Come like a full moon's night
That has been stolen by rain,
Dimmed grey, radiant but palled –
Moments when beauty creeps like pain,

I know the old futility of art,
But know as well the ladies and the lords
Of life are they who, knowing, feel
No call to blight that sense with words.

March Wind

The trees cry loud, "Oh, who will unchain us!"
  They gasp crying, but deep mold never stirs.
Never in this life shall they go whirling: –
  The storm's great burs.

My heart cries out, my heart is broken, Lady!
  What of after-years, with this deep pain sown?
Never to forget. But my heart is praying
  It had not known.

Port Dover, Ontario

I have written little more verse since "March Wind," and nothing I like so well. It makes the last of a group of about a dozen which may be printed some time... Mencken, I might remark cryptically, called poetry fallacies set to music.
  – *Raymond Knister. Reprinted in* Livesay "Memoir" xxiii.
  11.4.1924.

Letters to Lorne Pierce about
Windfalls for Cider

7.12.1925.

I am very glad of your interest in my poems. I should
appreciate your returning the magazines to me, as
unfortunately I have no other copies. The collection,
WINDFALLS FOR CIDER, while more or less
homogenous, would be made up of sections forming
a volume of such a size as the charmingly entitled
MORNING IN THE WEST which you published a
couple of years ago. It would represent, in reality, a
selected edition, as it is four years now since I first
gathered together a manuscript volume for a publisher
who, I subsequently discovered, wished to publish at
my expense.

17.06.1926.

I am glad that we have reached a point where we can
do something definite in regard to WINDFALLS FOR
CIDER…. I am rather surprised however that you
should expect me to assume responsibility for the
manufacture of the brochure, as I understood that it
was not a matter of a printing job, and that the Ryerson
Press in bringing out this series, was satisfied with the
indirect and direct returns. This of course was one
reason for my interest in the project. While I expect
never to make money out of poetry, I do not intend to
put a dollar of cash into it, and unless my poems can be

published in the regular way on their merits, I prefer to confine myself to reaching a public of whose interest I am sure through magazines. And I would prefer to have some of the expense of typings covered.

27.12.1926.

In regard to WINDFALLS FOR CIDER, it is now about a year since you received the present complete manuscript, and I think that you should definitely decide whether the House is to publish it....

Victor Lauriston, in the Chatham Daily News announced the publication of WINDFALLS FOR CIDER, saying along with other commendation, "...to my prophetic eye this little book is destined to be a greater landmark in Canadian literature than even Bliss Carman's 'Low Tide at Grand Pre' or Archibald Lampman's 'Among the Millet'. Other critics I expect would be similarly kind. It is too much perhaps to expect your House to subscribe to such a view, or at least to act in logical accordance with it, but you might at least persuade it that if only in view of my work to come, no money would be lost on this book, published in the ordinary way.

Perhaps though, what you need is new readers. What about my volunteering?

Letters to Lorne Pierce (Editor Ryerson Press)

Letter from A.J.M. Smith

12 February 1927.

Dear Mr. Knister,

I am writing to you to express my admiration of your stories and poems in THIS QUARTER and to ask you if you would be interested in the starting of a Canadian literary journal that should represent a break from the English tradition and the complacent inanities of the Canadian Author's Association. Surely there must be a few young writers in Canada who are capable of creating a literature that should be roughly complementary to the art of the Group of Seven. If we could get a group together and publish, say, a quarterly on fairly cheap paper I think we might do something towards hastening the advent of the long-awaited Canadian renascence: yourself, Morley Callaghan, E.J. Pratt, Merrill Dennison, Fred Jacob are the names that suggest themselves to me. I have been helping to edit for the past two years *The McGill Fortnightly Review* and have good cheap printers, a fairly loyal band of about three hundred subscribers in Montréal, and know one or two young men here who are doing interesting work and show promise of doing better. For myself, I am trying to write poetry, which is quickly becoming more subjective and more obscure, and have contributed to various American magazines – *The Dial, The Measure, The Nation, Voices*. Canadian magazines, with the exception of the *Forum* (and that is more political than literary) are hopeless. If you think this idea of a Canadian literary quarterly is a good one, or if you have any criticisms or suggestions to make will you be so good as to write me. Trusting that you will not regard this letter from an entire stranger as an intrusion,

I am,

Yours sincerely,

A.J.M. Smith

On Raymond Knister

30 August 1932 BORDER CITY STAR

J. Raymond Knister Lost Life
Monday Afternoon
Whilst Swimming in Lake St. Clair
at Stoney Point

———

Young Novelist Drops From
Sight While Swimming.

———

Was Well-Known
Short-Story Writer;
Born in Kent County

———

Raymond Knister, of Toronto, was drowned late yesterday afternoon near Stoney Point while swimming about a mile off shore. The body has not yet been recovered.

Born in County

Born in Rochester township about 32 years ago, he was the son of the late Robert W. Knister and Mrs. Knister. His father was prominent in Agricultural circles in Western Ontario, and one of the active workers in the Corn Growers Association for some years. The family home was in Essex County for some years and later in Kent County, south of Chatham.

For several weeks, Mr. and Mrs. Raymond Knister and their small daughter have been summering in the John Goatbe cottage at Willow Beach near Stoney Point. Yesterday afternoon he went out alone in a boat for a swim. He was about a mile off shore and in water about to his shoulders and Mrs. Knister was watching him from the beach when he jumped in for a swim. But he did not anchor the boat and it drifted away. In trying to swim after it, Mr. Knister perished.

Wife Alarmed

When Mr. Knister disappeared, his wife, frantic with fright, started to rush out into the water and then attracted attention of some fishermen nearby and they immediately went to the spot indicated by Mrs. Knister. They were unable to locate the body. The boat had drifted some distance out into the lake and was recovered four miles out.

He was known locally through publication of some of his works in The Border City Star.

He was one of Canada's most promising writers. A writer of short stories which are found in many modern collections, he edited a representative volume, "Canadian Short Stories."

Won $2,500 Prize Contest

He also wrote two novels, "White Narcissus" and "My Star Predominant," a novelized life of Keats; which won the $2,500 prize offered by an Ottawa publishing firm in 1931.

31 August 1932

To Mrs. Raymond Knister

Canada is greatly impoverished today. Her loss is the greatest since Carman left us. My deepest sympathies are with you Myrtle. Raymond was a loyal friend and the most brilliant son of soil of recent years. His spirit will live long among us.

Wilson MacDonald
Windermer, Ontario

30 August 1932

Raymond's star is still in the ascendant.

Edward Herman to Myrtle Knister

1 September 1932

Dear Mrs. Knister,

It is not a time to bother you, but I felt I must write. I heard the news of Raymond's death in Montréal and was terribly shocked; and grieved, as much for his sake, as for yours. Though I saw him only for a brief about three weeks ago, I was worried about his future, for the game of writing he had chosen has become such a precarious one these days. Moreover the stories he showed me I did not like so well as some of his previous work, and I told him so. But I have always been very interested in his work, it showed an inspired and profound mind. For this reason I would like to ask if there is anyone now in charge of his manuscripts – Pelham Edgar or Morley Callaghan – and if not, whether you would consent to let me see them. He has told me his plans about a play about his stories and poems and it might very well be that I could interest Mr. Eryrs of Macmillans in this publication. I should like very much to try. Doubtless you realise that such a venture would be a help to you, financially. My own interest is purely a personal remembrance, a wish to do something for so good a friend.

Could I see them? Perhaps I could come to Port Dover if there is too much to be put through the mails? What is your house address there?

Believe I am sincerely troubled by all this sorrow that has come to you. – are there no more intimate details of what actually happened than what appeared in the paper? Is there no hope of finding the body?

– Forgive me if I have interfered. It is because I would like my sympathy to be of some use. –

Very Sincerely yours,

Dorothy Livesay

In Loving Memory

Died

John Raymond Knister
August 29th, 1932
Aged 33 years

Funeral Services will be held at the United Church, Comber, Ont., Friday, September 2nd, 1932, at 2 p.m. followed by a service at the residence of Mr. Geo. Gamble, Port Dover, Ont., on Saturday, September 3rd, 1932, at 2 p.m. Interment in Port Dover Cemetery.

DIED

At Stoney Point, Lake St. Clair, Ont., on Monday, August 29th, 1932

John Raymond Knister

In his 34th year.

THE FUNERAL

Will take place from the residence of George Gamble, Main Street, Port Dover, on Saturday, September 3rd, 1932. Service at the house at 2.00 o'clock P.M., thence to the Port Dover Cemetery for interment.

Friends and acquaintances please accept this intimation.

2 September 1932

Dear Mrs. Knister;

Please accept my deepest sympathy. I was shocked
beyond measure on learning of the tragedy. My wife and
I feel with you in your grievous loss. The personal loss
to you and the children is, I know, beyond estimate and
the loss to Canada and to Canadian literature cannot be
reckoned. He had accomplished so much that was
worth-while in a few years, against the terrific odds
which confront a writer striving to maintain sincerity
and integrity in his work in this country, that he was
obviously one of our few genuine artists. The blind
eradication of that power and sensitivity is a stunning
and bewildering blow. I am glad that I was privileged to
meet him even for a few moments during his lifetime
and while I know that words are feeble things in the face
of such disaster I wanted you to know that our hearts
are with you at this time.

If there is any possible service I can render in a
professional capacity please accept my assurance that
I shall be only too happy to be of any help.

Yours very sincerely,

Leslie McFarlane

5 September 1932

Dear Mrs. Knister:

Friends of Raymond Knister, and they are everywhere
I am sure, are haunted by his tragic loss. To me the
sorrow is a great and personal one, and I assure you of
my profound sympathy.

Raymond came to me with his novel on Keats, and I
believe that I was among the first to praise it, hazarding
the opinion that it stood a good chance in the Graphic
Contest. Later he told me of their failure, and asked me
to assist in retrieving it, so that it might be published,
earn royalties, and above all protect the copyright. After
a great deal of correspondence I was able to purchase
the standing type, when the legal tangle, following
bankruptcy proceedings, had been cleaned up. I am
happy to think that he learned of our success before he
went. Later I had planned to send a contract, and settle
the date of publication.

He was anxious to find employment, and it was my
hope that we could make an opening at The Ryerson
Press. As you know, times are trying, and we were
anxious to hold our staff without dismissing any or
cutting salaries. To engage new help, in view of this,
was a real problem, yet I hoped to solve it. In the
meantime I promised some personal work, and he had
written accepting it. Raymond followed with another
letter, telling me of your camp, and expressing his
eagerness to get in to Toronto and at work. He wanted
an advance by return. The letter was addressed to my

office, and I, being out of town on vacation, did not receive it until a few days later, when I went in for an hour or so. I brought my mail to my cottage, and wrote him at once, saying that I was enclosing a cheque. The next morning I motored back to town to mail it, and when I reached my office word was awaiting me of his lamentable passing.

He was a rare spirit, and it would have given me great joy to help him.

I shall send the contract to you soon. Will you command me in any way?

Your friend,

Lorne Pierce

62 Delaware Ave.,
Toronto, Ontario, Canada,
Now. 27th, 1940.

Dear Mr. Gustafson, –

While I never knew Raymond Knister, I learned
something about him from a friend. He never published
a book of his verse, but probably would have done so.
He was about to return to Toronto to live when he was
drowned in the fall of 1932.

Immediately before his death a group of his poems
appeared in *The Canadian Forum* along with an article by
Leo Kennedy. I have copied out the group in its entirety.

A group of seven poems appeared in *The Midland* of
December 1921. Enough poems have appeared in
American poetry magazines to form a small volume but
they are still uncollected. He lived twenty years on an
Ontario farm, died at 32. He worked on *The Midland*,
also for *Poetry*. He placed short stories and poetry with
This Quarter (Paris, in the late twenties).

He had not become well-known and I am anxious to
help make sure that he doesn't get overlooked, which
might possibly happen as anthologists hereabouts show
a tendency to follow a well-worn track.

Yours sincerely,

W.W.E. Ross

13 October 1945

Owing to Dr. Pierce's limited time and health, he passed the task of preparing "Windfalls for Cider" to me, as well as the writing of the memoir on Raymond Knister, my mother and I knew him quite well in a literary way, so the main emphasis will be on that side of his life. There are however several biographical details which I need as background and also to explain why he wrote and how he wrote...

You will be interested to know that I read some of the poems in a lecture recently on Contemporary Canadians, and they were wonderfully well received. I read first the White Cat, but several more were asked for. I think the book should become really popular and of great literary interest.

Letter from Mrs. Duncan Macnair to Mrs. Myrtle Grace (nee Knister)

November 1945

I am startled to discover that in the little time since
Raymond was drowned, (1932-3) a legend has sprung
up that is as utterly cock-eyed as you'd expect one to be
in a century. I was working on the Montréal Herald the
day the news came, and promptly some mugs who
worked on that feeble sheet started nodding their heads
wisely and saying, 'Ah yes, Knister, a suicide of course.'
Presumably with as little basis, similar specimens did
the same thing in Ontario. If anyone was close to
Raymond Knister in his last year, I was, and I will swear
on as high a stack of Bibles as you elect that the man
drowned. What is more, I shall be happy to go into print
and fight the first published inference that such warn't
the case. I shall fight you, if you like. And I've a docket
of evidence and argument as long as your arm. When
Raymond Knister drowned, with his wife screaming at
some lounging oafs to go to his rescue, he was on the
way *up*. He was through with the crazy Graphic
 business; lawyers had nicked a good piece of his prize
money but he did have the bulk of it. We had just read
the proofs of the Keats novel. Macmillan had made a
deal with him to serve as a reader at a price. Economically
he was in the clear. What's more, he felt, as he wrote me
from Ontario (I was still in the depression in Quebec), all
his creative powers quickening. Everything was going
good for that guy and he knew it. He said it. He wrote it
too me. These are some of the reasons why I shall be

most happy to knock the block off the first sensationalist
who starts construing his tragic death as self-destruction.

Leo Kennedy to Dorothy Livesay

16 June 1949

To me there are two mysteries about Raymond. One,
of course, was the mystery of his death which still
depresses me when I think about it. What could I have
done that I did not do? And I wonder why, but no one
can say. Certainly his work was done, at least done in a
matter far beyond his years, and his influence is abiding.
The second mystery is how a boy so young, from a farm,
almost without academic training, should naturally
move into his rightful place beside the most creative and
progressive minds of his time, how could he unerringly
place his finger on the great long before it became
recognized and point out the shoddy even while it was
being acclaimed.

I have changed the reference to Morley Callaghan. I
agree with you that it might sound unfair. I put in its
place Sir Gilbert Parker, who is a classic example of a
man who sold out to the commercial.

Letter from Lorne Pierce to Myrtle Grace

19 May 1949
Miss Margaret V. Ray,
Associate Librarian,
The Library,
Victoria University
Toronto

Dear Miss Ray:

I did not get to know Raymond Knister until shortly
before his death which came as a great shock to me
because on his last night in Toronto he came to my
house and stayed until the small hours, urging me to
keep on reading a partly finished manuscript of mine,
later published as "Think of the Earth".

His eagerness to know what other writers were
doing and his encouraging constructive comments on
their work were indicative of a generous attitude toward
competitors which unfortunately is all too rare.

While it was obvious that he had read widely and
was alert to current trends, his conversation was free of
sophistication and artiness, being redolent rather of
earth and growth and weather and simple souls.

In *My Star Predominant*, of course he was dealing
with another world, another time, and with the tortured
complex nature of a young poet of immense gifts. His
study of Keats, however, although dealing with works of
imagination of the highest order, matches in the humility
of his treatment the humility he shows, mixed with
exalted egotism, in the nature of Keats. There is a fine
passage of dialogue which paraphrases the famous letter
regarding the "negative capability" of the poet, and one

feels as one reads that Knister was not so much creating something as absorbing and revealing what he had learned of Keats' creative achievement.

There is a slightly archaic tone throughout the book which helps to carry us back to the tune and the people who were drawn into the circle of Keats' life. Few Canadians have attempted such a task, let alone carried it through to so satisfactory a conclusion.

The only other work of Knister's which I can remark on with any degree of familiarity is an unpublished manuscript titled "The Innocent Man" which he left with me to read. It was our intention to have a session on it later, but I never saw him again.

The manuscript, which I turned over to Dr. Lorne Pierce, is of novelette length and concerns a convict. If I remember correctly the story takes place entirely within the prison walls. There is little action, but I can still recall the trueness of the dialogue between the cell-mates. It is close to being typical of so many manuscripts written by Canadians whose independence prevents them from following leads or pandering to a market.

Had he lived, Knister's robust mind, generous heart, and exceptional gifts, would undoubtedly have contributed in an outstanding way to Canadian literature.

Sincerely,

Bertram Brooker

Morley Callaghan on Raymond Knister

Raymond was – well, I would say, a rather good-looking man. He had a sensitive face and his forehead was enlarged by a kind of premature baldness which was really just at the front of his head which gave him a very dignified and rather an interesting intellectual appearance – but I'll tell you the peculiar quality about Raymond – he had very interesting eyes – they used to irritate me a little, these eyes of Raymond's – they were good eyes and in a sense they were the eyes of a writer but they were also the eyes of an enormously self-conscious man. Now you might be talking to Raymond – say – if you were in a room with six or seven people – and then you would notice that Raymond was not talking directly to you – he would be talking to you – but these eyes of his – you know – they'd be wandering all around the place – the eyes of either a nervous man or a self-conscious man or a man intent on knowing what was going on behind him, in back of him, in front of him, so you always had the feeling that he was in four or five places.... Raymond knew what was going on in London and New York, Paris and so on. I couldn't figure the guy out – I mean – this was what was strange to me about Raymond – how did this boy, off the farm – you know – have this taste and understanding about writing? I have no idea how he got this way – this was what so strange about him among Canadian writers. He was the only guy I knew in Toronto at that time – who, you know, that I might do a story and I could take it to Raymond and I would know that Raymond was reading this story just as someone in New York or Paris might read it and his judgment was just as good. Raymond *knew* what was *good!* In any time and in any period, these men are very rare – and Raymond had this peculiar taste and understanding about literature....

And this is where we sort of went two different ways – I was interested in talking with Raymond, but Raymond sort of knew everybody. He had this hunger to know writers – you know – so he would go off visiting Charles G.D. Roberts and Wilson MacDonald and Mazo de la Roche and so on, and he'd come back reporting to me about them...

Excerpt taken from CBC Radio Show "The Farmer Who Was Also Poet."
Produced by John Wood and Allan Anderson. 19 July 1964.

Arthur Stringer came to Toronto in November 1928 and the Writers' Club invited him to speak. This drew a large crowd and excited unusual interest. Arthur Stringer was not only what women called "a gorgeous hunk of a man" but he was outstanding among Canadian authors of his day for sales and earnings. There was secret envy in the Toronto writing world, mingled with open admiration for his achievements. (25)

Raymond Knister and his wife occupy the suite just above us. I am constantly hearing the intonation and the sentence rhythm, though never the words, of a Canadian author, as I sit in my living room at my portable type-writer. Before I finish these notes I am sure to hear the low vocal vibration, and the step of his foot immediately above me. When Raymond starts typing (on a portable, like my own) a subdued clicking is also audible. Thus I can hear the slow growth of a Canadian novel that, for all I know, may set the literary Thames on fire. (28-9).

from Literary Friends. *Wilfrid Eggleston. Borealis Press, Ottawa 1980.*

Collected Poems

Edited by Dorothy Livesay, 1949.

Raymond Knister

Ploughman's Song

Turn under, plow,
My trouble;
Turn under griefs
And stubble.

Turn mouse's nest,
Gnawing years;
Old roots up
For new love's tears.

Turn plow, the clods
For new thunder.
Turn under, plow,
Turn under.

29 April 1925. Northwood, Ontario.

Night Whistling

Serene, mounting, as a bird's far cry –
  In hour when birdsong would be dear,
Fleet-shapen notes from the silent pavements,
  A young man's whistling makes night clear.

Long it hangs in the bare tree boughs,
  Lingers yet in the ear a little while
Till even tranquil memory's allayed, –
  Comes back in sleep across the lenient mile.

On "Ploughman's Song"

Deacon of Saturday Night read my book of poems and of his own accord asked for "Ploughman's Song" for that Literary Section of which he is so proud. It is the only place in Canada I would have a poem of mine. It would mean nothing at all to have a poem in any other, because they print so much hokum

— *Raymond Knister. Letter to Elizabeth Frankfurth. 27.03.1927.*

The shape of "Ploughman's Song" is slender, the lines brief; the pared down, spare form matches the simplicity of the language used. But because, in contrast, the resonances created are complex, the effect achieved is one of great concentration. Knister coordinates the tension between the contained and the continuous.

— *Joy Kuropatwa. Raymond Knister and His Works. 18.*

Raymond Knister

Poems, Stories, and Essays

Edited by John Moss, David Arnason, & John Sorfleet, 1975.

So Long Lives This... (To An Unheeding One)

It is when I look at Autumn's
Mocking with red tongues forgotten
Summer's passion, with slender air
Fooling Winter's arms,

Wondering a little – after all –
Letting Autumn tell me without wincing
There'll be other Autumns, more amber
To wail downing I must watch –

I think that girls
Like you should not remember
Or see these things;
Be wise and keep away from the windows:

Rain, you told me,
Has splashed through the screen,
Beaten to the carpet rose-petals
From the vase beside your bed.

Iowa City, Iowa

Whip-Poor-Will in North Woods

Dark cry in the dim
Of mellow night
Leaves memory a siesta...
To return
Hemming dream about us.

WHIP
POOR
WILL!

A wing
Over lakes resting,
And the ghost-trees
Who do not forget
Hot stormlight
Muffling stars.

Blenheim, Ontario

Woman Reading Poetry

Paper like wisps of snow
On the granite blue of Cat's hair:
I cut the pages
Unminding this selvage of dreams sifting
That might have known me.

But one steals toward my soul,
I chanting wake, and you, my Cat,
Slip silken from my lap; and on the footstool,
In a lull look up from slanted topaz
Opening eyes:
A metal god of China come
Across seas that reach to music.

Blenheim, Ontario

A New Year's Reverie

The wind of winter's night comes sighing
   Through the white-trimmed cedars tall,
Through the wind-brushed cloud-mane flying,
   A full white moon, grandly sailing lets fall
Light and shade to the prostrate earth.
   A rusty windmill's sudden loud complaining
Accentuates the utter dearth
   Of sound... The light is softly shifting, waning,
Now that the cloud-veil slips between;
   But a far, white roof is shining –
That rat-tat-tat of "Emma Gee's" must mean
   Another charge at dawn. The shrill whining
Of "Whistling Jimmy" is a torture to the ear,
   Only to be outdone by the unavailing cries
Of the stricken, which, intermittently heard, wear
   To the soul. But Time, as well as Death, flies:

Over the bags at dawn! The weighing
  Life in hand and flinging it past the low
Fear of fear... But now moonlight, soft, allaying,
  Equal exposure makes of friend and foe.

"L'Envoi"

Dear Lord, one moon looks down upon us!
One ache consumes the hearts of all!
And, though we err, do thou not frown upon us,
But let us, tempted by rage-rent hearts to fall,
Cease for one day this fear-born hate,
Lest the coming years deny
The hope of peace, lest our most hoped for fate
Obdured by our wilful blindness pass us by.

16 January 1918.

Against the Years

I would undo the years with their undoing,
Little and brief as these thoughts, I
Consider
And though a cloud lifts to show
Blackness,
Trees purr remembering the tempest,
I am not cajoled and if life relieves me I shall protest
Its outrage. A mouse can squeal
Before it runs, and a crow
With quick eye sweeps the sky
As each time the quick beak picks the bone.
Man, feigning confidence to charm a wildness
That destroys him, knowing only
Enough to be dizzy, sometimes forgets to peer, roar,
tremble,
Reach – and is left for dead.
If he does not die of being left for dead,
Rising on elbow he may syllable his outrage
And die so.
Thomas Hardy
Wearing still his hat,
Looking through the pane
At the Winter's day of life
Others find so bracing.
Chekhov, Anton listening
Letting a whisper of leaves in moonlight
Tell him the soul is immeasurable
Though people talk.
Sherwood Anderson telling his soul other souls

Are souls like it.
James contriving anodyne
In embellishment,
Proust hoping a music
Because he has deafened himself.
Conrad contriving grave diapasons
From flying discords of his world.
These, as though there were no such thing
As death, and nothing else but
Death.
Anatole France besotting himself on irony
Because love will not take him
Or let him go –
These
Minister to my song,
Revenge too brief and long.

Windfalls for Cider [1983]

Edited by Joy Kuropatwa, 1983.

The Humorist

I am written of as a great humorist,
A jester with life,
A laugher at men.
People say, "I have heard him speak,
He's just like his picture.
He tells his jokes with such side-aching gravity
I nearly died. You ought to hear him,
So much better than his books, him looking so solemn."
All my life I've wanted to write
Something sad, grim and pitiful.
I just took up this side-tickling humour to start with,
To gain the public ear.
I've always been going to begin
To tell the world of its goalless gropings,
Its tortive mazeful stumblings,
But now I'm too old to try.
Poe, Hardy and Dostoyevsky
Are my prophets,
And people say
I'm another Juvenal, Rabelais, Cervantes,
Anyone they think their listeners have not read.

20 January 1921. Blenheim, Ontario.

Superfluous Words on a Drive

Now moon glamours the lake
And mothers the sleep of trees
That breathe a little and wake
And clutch at misty blanket-seas.

Girl, I know that you see:
Let's not pretend to be strangers;
Night's clement, and we
Should not seek inept dangers.

Lonely all night long
Timidly little waves caress
Withdrawn shores in a song
They never can quite express.

Love, (there's no other word!)
Promise to remember well:
Together we have known and heard
The moon's old casual spell.

Blenheim, Ontario.

The Quick and the Dead

I stood in a graveyard,
   All the tombs were still
And the moon stared blandly
   Over the hill.

With you beside me
   They were less than stone,
Till laughing we kissed,
   And then it was done:

There was nothing but slept,
   And yet I knew
As they flashed coldly,
   Each one hated – you!

Chicago, Illinois. See alternate version.

Cinquain: Pattern

The sleet
Through warp of wind....
Is the pattern profoundly weird as these
Sharp guesses to
My heart.

Blenheim, Ontario. 4 April 1924. See alternate version.

On "The Quick and the Dead"

Here, a contrast is developed between love and pleasure on the one hand, and the cold finality of death on the other. At the physical centre of the poem, love as a force of life has the power to transform surrounding gravestones into "less than stone." Then, "laughing we kissed," and the spark of procreation kindles dread antagonism of the dead toward the living.

> —*Alexander Kizuk.* A Reassessment of Early Twentieth-
> Century Canadian Poetry in English. *244.*

Because They Are Young

There is plenty enough of sorrow
Before the years have been told,
Why must young lovers borrow
A loaf which should feed the old?

The old should eat and be reconciled,
They should count the crumbs and weep
That ever they were beguiled
By dream foreshadowing sleep.

They have seen the stars and sun,
Have clung to the pulse of night.
They know there is nothing, not one
More than a sound and a sight.

They know that the soul goes lonely
Through shifting mazes of years,
That the call they hearken is only
Laughter and tears.

The old can remember sorrow
They bore for a little while,
How it promised a shining morrow...
They rest, they listen and smile.

But youth has the lost quick aching,
The sweetness bitter with thirst,
And longs for the dear awaking
Though the clear day be accursed.

The passioned young should know
What phantoms are they, girl and boy:
And how the visioned seed they sow
Is mere insufferable joy.

Jarvis Street, Toronto. 2 November 1926.

Snowfall

Floating and sifting
Into earth's eyes;
Dimming their wildness
With tinted phases.

Into her ears
Sifting and floating;
Numbing the discords
With a tone unheard.

Muffling the thrum
Of pulses, the fever
With pale bright sleep.

Sifting and floating ...
I am earth's dreaming.

See alternate version and additional version.

Unpublished Poetry
and Alternate Versions

From the Raymond Knister Collection in the William Ready Archives (McMaster), Imogen Givens Personal Files, and Victoria Archives (University of Toronto).

The Longest June Evening

Wind out of nowhere dragged the blue trees,
Blue fields.
Slammed doors; you fled from room
To room laughing, shutting windows
Laughing; but before you came to our room,
The bed was soaked, the screen spraying.
Then – your stole upon the veranda bench,
(That veranda bench!)
You held the door, I dashed back in a flash,
Wet to the skin; you pushing the brutal door.
We cried aloud from room to room.
Kissed, and before we knew, it went
With a last spattering hail.
The fields were green again, bitter,
The ineffectual calm sun setting, as before,
Water ran in the ditch, ditches in corn-rows,
Sheets in the yard.
Then the fireflies, do you remember....
Remember the fireflies? Your eyes
Grew dark, calm, unteased by
The pricking fireflies everywhere
Out of the blind of night, out of the bush
The dark gardens, the trembling oats field....
We sat, listening to the little words,
And saying a few remembered.
Do you remember?

22 June 1925

In a Conservatory

Is it so much, that being old,
One knows the buds one would not buy
Not worth the hoarding of this gold
 – For fires to remember flowers by?

Early version of "Speculation in a FlowerMarket." See alternate version.

Nellie Rackerfield

She was the teammate of Lide,
Nearly as big, and snappy
In action, always wanting to be ahead,
So that a green driver might kill her.
But her pedigree was not that of Lide's.
For that matter she had none.
So her colts were allowed to run wild,
And one died before a veterinarian was got.
She became old quickly,
And clover-poisoning made ugly
Her large white face with its small nostrils,
Her white-haired legs.
She passed, sold, from hand to hand.

See alternate version in "A Row of Stalls."

Madrigal

Oh, by what word can be gainsaid
   Old love that makes the past seem strange
Yet far and sad, waylaid
    By grislier strangeness in future's bourne,
What word inuring us to pang of change?
    In you that word is born,
        that word is born.
Hearkening on your unspeaking mouth
  Its echo, brings love's promises to drouth,
         love's promises to drouth

Blenheim, Ontario

Quarry

Your eyes would only joke in all that hour,
  They'd tell me not a thing;
If I pursued to find their covert out –
  There only flashed a wing.

And when I rose and made to come away
  You left the others, cold.
But in the hall your eyes veered back,
  Your slow hand shyly told.

Blenheim, Ontario

Raymond Knister

Sonnet: A Soldier

Why should he die in all his splendid youth,
Who might, and with best grace, have savoured life
Through many nook-shot vales of fancy, rife
With deepest music of the vibrant truth;
In whom did seem enthroned such gentle ruth
With justice and forbearance all in wove,
And yet so cunningly, fresh treasure trove
They seem to those whose eyes his death renew'th.

Ask rather why the moon should draw the tide,
Compelling to its will man's feeble bark,
Than such a soul to follow and abide
Should trust itself, and boldly to embark,
To gaze within the eye of Time for guide
And dare long sleep amid the dreary dark.

December 1919.

Spring-Flooded Ditches

Josh Naylor breaks off neat lengths of
    telephone-pole shadows.

The yellow-dripping spokes of his buggy turn
    in long-rolling splash down the clay ruts.

The moon shows her face, finds things unchanged,
    and petulant shades her stare,

Looking a second at Clym Norton's bridge as it
    hangs on the lift of the ditch.

Wind upon the telephone-wires, wash of the ditch
    about the necks of last fall's weeds,
    you make a strange music for Josh,
    to whom music is strange.

Telephone-poles ring forth down the ditches
    far ahead and behind him,
    with dullness, with deep resonance.

Poles and wires, you become in his musings
    the thrumming and well-spaced years
    as he puddles along and past you.

Raymond Knister

The Unattainable

I rose, for the moon had risen,
  And said, for only the sky had caught my glance,
And my thoughts forgotten their wonted prison –
  Only a will of bird-song enchained mine ear –
Surely, surely it is mine, the spirit of that trance
And will bear me within in inward prison over grief and fear?

So spake I, then 'gan think of night
  And truce not all, not all, ignoble, counting
Of the slain in that day's causeless-seeming fight;
  Dreams of the changing vision, that only when, meseems, it nears,
Became impalpable, leaving spent day for broken until, mounting
A far off, I glimpse again, that strand of song through all the mingled
years.

2 February 1920. Blenheim, Ontario.

La Vie

La vie est brève
Un peu d'amour,
Un peu de rêve
Et pais – bonjour!

La vie est vaine,
Un peu d'espair,
Un peu de [harne?],
Et puis – bon soir!

Life (from the French)

Brief is life:
With dreams it may,
Perchance, be rife,
And then – Away!

Life is wain;
A little hope,
And hate insane,
And then – the rope.

To One Lost

Your voice was in the air last night,
  It was strange to have you near;
The rooms were filled with laughter and light
  And no one seemed to hear.

From the mockery at the window I turned away
  And did not close it out.
But how impossible to chatter and be gay, –
  Your voice in my heart and without

Iowa City, Iowa.

Lachrymae Rerum

There is no sleep, but tossing
  There is no rest, but woe
Ah, when shall cease that crossing
  Whence all visions flow!

There is no grief but waiting,
  Waiting through the years;
And no relief in mating
  Sorrow's sighs with tears.

There's no respite from questing
  On quests without an end:
(To follow each behesting
  Is all the gods may send.)

Ah, when shall come a ceasing
  Of woes and wasting wars,
And the heart may find it easing,
  Night, and the wide-set stars!

1917

Dragonflies at Noon

Dragon – flies at noon.
D D D D D D D
Dragon – f f f f flies at noon noon
Dragon f f f f f fl lies fl lies
l l l l lies lies

Hand-written, playful concrete poem from Knister's journal beneath a plot outline for "Mist-Green Oats". Written December 1921. Knister, it might be noted, published a review of E E Cummings for the Border Cities Star *in 1922.*

Raymond Knister

Conundrum

And it is to remember
That you are loaned a little while
To quickness, softness, and a smile
The future will dismember

Is it in the afternoon
Mirage of my parched throat
That you sat singing in a boat,
That dusk is gliding soon

In wide grey eyes as though
No pain were on the green,
Mist on the river never seen
And silent-floating we might go...

As to the moonrise you could smile
(Oh now, is that a debt,
Does memory wisely promise yet?)
And aches be fused a little while.

Walkerville, Ontario. See "And is it to remember" on page 164.

An Old Wooden Windmill

Mornings I used to stand proudly,
Vane a white arm out-thrown derisively to the
            chasing breeze.
Long wings twirled with languid and throbbing swiftness.
Afternoons
I peeked across pasture and bush-land, between the trees,
Burnished silver until sun-down.

Came nights of infuriate storm,
Years in the nights,
Frenzied whirlings through the long dark:
The rag-wheel broken.

Now,
No mercy from caprice of clouds,
Of any whipping breeze to twitch the leaves.
The wind's wild will is mine.
Dark and gaunt-framed,
Blue and veering in the day,
In the night
With rusty, sudden,
Loud complainings
I 'fright the birds, asleep.

Blenheim, Ontario. See alternate version.

Did We Need the Rain

Did we need the rain
  In the night to tell
Beauty waits in pain
  Or love's tears? But the rain fell
Quietly to roofs,
  Kindly to earth's men.
And dark air knew the longing
  Their lips spread in vain.

Soft rain waits in the dark
  Like an old love
In memory to mark
  What tides the moon may move
Even the leaves have told
  What lips deny;
The sky draws closer
  To list earth's sigh.

O love, shall we find
  Comfort of song
Beyond the tapestry of mind
  Close-held so long,
Or hide our bodies
  From gentleness of rain,
Even as our souls lost
  In a mist of pain.

Now Me

As surely comes the hour we dare not face
And I who know that you are thinking now
"We dance like two lost leaves flung from the branch
To settle soft in music's windy chase
Like soul's lost in a vast immense embrace
Like our lost selves, in fire

Handwritten on back of typeset "The Life in Letters." Notes suggest "Now Me" was never finished.

Liberty Nut-Cracker No.1

A young fellow whose first name was Jim,
Went down to the sea for a swim,
    When a shark took a hunch
    It was time for his lunch.
Reader, and then? His chances were slim.

Liberty Nut-Cracker No. 2

An exceedingly dry man from Maine,
Once lost his best girl on a train,
    And this loss so unnerved him
    That when dinner was served him,
He called for a chaser – in vain.

Serene, mounting as a bird's far cry

Serene, mounting as a bird's far cry, –
An hour when bird-song would be dear,
Fleet-shapen notes from the silent pavements,
A young man's whistling makes night clear.

Long it hangs in the bare tree boughs,
      Lingers yet in the ear a little while
      Until the tranquil memory's allayed, –
            Come back in sleep, across the lenient mile.

4 April 1924

For One Quick

I stood in a graveyard
    All the tombs were still,
And the moon stared redly
    On the edge of the hill.

There was nothing but slept,
    And yet I knew
As light flashed coldly,
    They all hated you.

4 April 1924. See alternate version "The Quick and the Dead."

Pattern

The sleet drives strands
Through weft of wind
Is the pattern
Not less endless
Than
Guesses to my heart.

4 April 1924. Alternate version below.

Pattern: Fabric

Sleet weft
Through warp of wind...
Homespun less weirdly enduring than these
Sharp guesses through
My heart?

To J.A.C. On Receipt of a Portrait

Dear Chester, though I like your art,
I can't but see, (and who could not)
This "counterfeit presentment" is but part
Of what, meseems, I needs must seem.
My best is far too kindly caught
And shadowed forth with many a ray
From your mind's star to flatter truth,
Yet I'm not one to wish it other, since we part
Never, perchance, to meet again in youth.
For still, despite man's wiles, the world is wide,
Still Fate and the immitigable years divide

March 1920. Toronto General Hospital.

A Foiled Coquette

I know that where you stay
    Safe from unwanted arms,
Is little peace, for all you say,
    And no less of love's alarms.

For if your will was not to save,
    Nor mine was all to bless,
I am in exile from the nave
    Of Dian's temple not the less.

And when you did not know
  Your mind you should have said
(In silence) "There let him go,
  But my heart shall not be led."

You should: but I am wondering now
  When I might have longed, –
I only wonder, hearing you avow
  That it is I've been wronged.

In the Spring Dusk, Gazing Above the Trees

Whither the clouds
Steaming level, forging slowly,
In silence, with spaces,
From the sunset's purple harbour-town
Through searchlight gleams,
Beneath a vain slim moon,
Steering by pharos-gleam of star –
Forging level,
Steaming slowly
To what unseen ports
And glimmer of simulated dawn.

See alternate version. Alternate title "Over Trees and Spring Dusk."

Yet Again

How should I dream again
   Now that I've known your eyes
Sea-green to blue or misty, –
   I'm grown deliriously wise.

I have grown drunk a-dreaming
   In days before you came
And learned from that but little
   For now it is the same:

I'll never know hereafter
   (It is the way of dreams.)
The faërie your eyes hold,
   The mystery in their gleams,

'Till I essay once more
   The sorcery in their wells
And be as wise as ever
   With what no word tells.

Iowa City, Iowa. Very similar to "Sea-Blue Eyes" on page 82.

Until, Still Young

"Put not your trust in women,"
  I heard a wise man say,
Nor hearkened, for I saw him
  Not wise, but worn and gray.

I laughed – Oh, many a time:
  The words were not forgot!
I laughed until today
  When laughter helps me not.

"Put not your trust in women,"
  I'll say it too, and nod;
And laughing boys will spare me
  Belief, and old pain's rod.

And I shall always say it
  Till I am old, like him:
Till then I shall content me
  With woman's every whim.

For though till then I swear
  With oaths of every size,
I'd sooner not believe me,
  Though then I should be wise.

There is no sleep but tossing

There is no sleep but tossing,
There is no rest; but woe;
Oh, where shall come the Crossing
Whence all visions flow!
There is no grief but waiting,
Waiting through the years;
And no relief in mating
Sorrow's sighs with tears.

There's no respite from questing,
On quests without an end;
(To follow each behesting
Is all the Gods may send).
Ah, when shall come a Crossing
Of woes and wasting wars,
And the heart may find it easing,
Night, and the wide set stars!

Dream

"Life   .   .   .   .   .
Life!   .   .   .   .   .
Ah, Life!"   .   .   .   .
He moaned, dreaming,
And awoke, seeing,
Dying.

Snowfall

Floating and sifting
Into her eyes;
Dimming their wildness
With tinted phases.

Into her ears
Sifting and floating:
Numbing the discords
With a tone unheard.

Muffled the thrumming
Of pulses, the fever
With pale bright sleep.

Sifting and floating. . .
I am earth's dreaming.

Unpublished manuscript version found in 1 August 1920 letter to Miss Louise Nicholl, of The Measure. *Blenheim, Ontario. See alternate versions*

The Ploughman

All day I follow
Watching the swift dark furrow
That curls away before me.
And care nor for skies nor upturned flowers,
At the end of the field
Look backward
Ever with discontent:
A stone, a root, a random thought
Has warped the line of that furrow –
And urge my horses round again.

But the next one shall be straighter.
Every furrow shall be straighter than the last.
Sometimes even before the row is finished
I must look backward;
To find when I come to the end
That there I swerved.

Unappeased I leave the field,
Expectant, return:
Every new land,
Every new furrow may be the goal.

The horses are patient.
When I tell myself
The ultimate sought for turning
Is before my share,
They must give up their rest.

Some day, some day, be sure,
I shall turn the furrow of all my hopes.
Bust I shall not, doing so, look backward.

Blenheim, Ontario. See alternate version.

August Night

What is the word that night is saying,
      Dark night, still?
The curtains waver, but the unheard voice
      Makes no pause at the sill.

The room does not know it has heard
      But I know,
My heart listening, wild with the word
      Murmured too low.

I shall hear what the nights have told,–
      Another night
When this heart is the word it is speaking
      In clouds' hush or starlight...

Blenheim, Ontario

Raymond Knister

And is it to remember

And is it to remember
    Love cannot grow old
That we turn each ember,
    Blow a breath that's cold.

With little words and sighings
    For love that may be gone
Like the tremulous flyings
    Of nestlings in the dawn?

They are chilly little words
    And we fear that they
For all longing, like birds
    Too shall veer away.

But if Love seems gone now
    It's only we are lost,
And her unwithered trow
    Glows beyond this frost:

It's never Love grows old
    And we should remember
As hearts grow cold
    It's only <u>our</u> November.

Iowa City, Iowa. See "Conundrum" on page 142.

A New Heaven and a New Earth

Prose and Selected Emphemera

The Dominion of Canada! It is hard to be sceptical, not to think that there are infinite spiritual possibilities in a land as huge and undeveloped as this, open to the variety and potency of influences which bear upon it, heritage to the racial amalgam already emergent.

– Raymond Knister, "Canadian Letter"

Sidewalks of Toronto

One

A bright orange balloon floating from the open window of an attic. It hangs there, with no visible means of restraint, bobbing brightly up and down... A youth in a fur coat and no hat or cap, riding a bicycle swiftly... A boy running valiantly after truck. He catches it and swings his feet from the ground... A girl wearing only dark clothes: dark-blue coat with a cape flying as she walks in the wind... Messenger boy riding a wheel, with rubber hip-boots... A truck-load of iron pipes, chained so that they do not rattle. Borne by a silent new motor, cushioned by springs, they traverse the city faster and more comfortably than iron pipes would have dreamed of doing a few years ago... A restaurant opposite a police station. Two burly arms of the law enter and towering above the patrons hunched on the stools, order sandwiches and pots of tea, and carry them across the street to the station... A man carrying in his hand a nickel model of a horse's hoof... Sign in Church Street: "Poultry and Produce."... A truck-load of charcoal in paper bags, a red rag tied to its after part... A man with a bunch of rhubarb leaves loosely wrapped in paper... Guns and hunting-knives still filling two large windows... A man in battered clothes and battered face, on Bloor Street, whistling blithely, eyes raised to the morning sky... The same man in the afternoon on downtown Bay Street, still whistling as he marches through the crowds... A tiny woman with blowsy hair

and skirts that touch the ground, staring through a
plateglass window up at a winter wrap, Sale Price,
$650... Two automobiles backing out of their parking
places on each side of the street. They rush toward each
other like charging bulls for a few yards, then charge
ahead, without either driver seeming aware of the other.

Two

A one-horse democrat bearing a cider mill and a chicken-
crate... A long wooden extension-ladder to the roof of an
old Jarvis Street mansion. New eaves glittering in the
sun around half the house... Sign: Lum Yet, Laundry...
Signboard, a carefully notched handsaw and the legend:
Tools Sharpened and Repaired... A woman wrapping a
shawl about the neck and mouth of a child as they are
getting into a streetcar... The windows of a third-storey
room open, the curtains flying out, and the lights on, in
the early afternoon... Danforth Avenue. Something of
Main Street clings to it. Saturday afternoons, nights,
Sunday nights it is thronged with natives of the nearby
residential sections, like the home-town Main Street on
a Saturday night... Except that there is no line of
automobiles parked at almost right angles along either
curb... The patterns of light in the ravines. Twin rows
of pearls winding off along the valley road toward
Rosedale... The roadway along Danforth, then the
cross-street beneath with its bridge over the ravine, then

the road in the ravine, far below, bare now, comparatively, among the denuded trees... An old, cement or stone mill-like structure glimmering in the half-light, perched n the edge of the slope. It seems to have no doors, until you see a broad shallow opening, closed by a sort of portcullis which lowers... Standing over the edge of the ravine it looks like a feudal keep... But the valley is quiet and bright under the lights. No automobiles, no one else walking the valley road, under the bare trees... At a gradual slope the road carries you to a little park, a stretch of grass overlooking Yonge Street... In the side streets west the houses seem cramped and frozen together. No grass before them, nothing between the sidewalk and the curb... A youth comes out of a house, highly dressed, walking buoyantly. Three urchins sitting on the curb opposite watch him, snickering: "Whoa there! Whoa!"

Three

An electric coupe with a large dog looking out of the window before the driver; so far that it looks as though he might fall. He barks and acts as the klaxon... An old man in a side street carrying rolled blankets from door to door. He does not pause long when there is no response... A little organ-grinder and his wife on Bloor Street. The briskly plaintive tones of the organ... No monkey in evidence... New buildings going up, with

a narrow roofed and railinged passageway for
pedestrians... The remarkable patience of pedestrians
passing such a place month after month, and always
having to stop or steer off into a switch to let each other
past... A raised automobile driveway where cars are
repaired from beneath, and a dog sleeping on one of the
tracks... Laundry sign: Lum You... Sherbourne Street.
Repairs to the paving and the car-tracks. Sand and dust
among the bricks... A long runabout, tearing down the
empty street at noon-hour, raising a swirl of dust which
the wind carries... A newspaper lifted high, soaring. An
old man peers anxiously into a yellow garbage box at a
corner. Perhaps he was putting the paper there when the
wind took it away from him... A streetcar. Six or eight
chilly strangers riding through the night. The car stops.
The conductor calls something to the motorman, and
goes forward. The motorman opens his door and goes
out. Comes back after five minutes. Men in the front
part go to the window and look out... Two in the rear
who have paid and passed the conductor mutter and
fidget uncomfortably. Finally they go to the head of the
car. A huge moving van with an equally huge trailer lies
diagonally across the tracks like a whale athwart a
launch. A tall blue policeman puts his shoulder to the
rear of the trailer, goes ahead, comes back and shoves
again. The motor man appears and shoves too. Finally
the whole caravan begins to creep round a car parked
at the curb, and gets clear of the tracks. Motorman,
conductor and passengers take their old places, grinning
at each other.

Four

Noon. A side street. A team of heavy draught horses
hitched to a moving-van. The driver throws blankets
over their backs, and taking the bits out of their mouths,
attaches feed bags... A man comes out of a tea-room with
a steaming mug. Not hot punch... A man with a red
muffler... An urchin in a man's cap with ear-mufflers
and a man's vest, darts into a department-store entrance
behind the back of a pompous doorman... A man on
downtown Yonge Street with an uncovered basket of
apples. Crowds jostle, a newsboy yells, "Hey, Mister,
give me an apple!"... A woman wearing a black fur
coat turns into a women's tailoring shop with a brown
fur coat on her arm... The confirmed jaywalked. When
he steps blithely into the traffic and pauses between
rows of automobiles, the traffic policeman ignores him
as completely as he ignores the signs... There may be
time for the funeral... Front Street, westward; brick
roadway and walks, yellow dust and high wind. Boxes
of buildings, grimly staring. Everything passing over
this pavement rattles... The long bridge over the railway
yards. Trains passing beneath belch smoke and noise...
The Lake, which seems removed from this dirt and noise
and huge structures, because near shore its water is not
so clear. But farther out, it might be the sky, removed
and far... And at this moment boatless... The Island
silent and removed as a picture... Coming back to the
travelled ways, the same crowd is milling toward or
from lunch. Well-dressed, buoyant, savouring the keen
fresh air; or thoughtful, depressed, lagging... An old

man holding out pencils with a yellow sock over his hand... Few men smoking on the street, fewer using toothpicks reminiscently... Next to a bargain-counter, a popular restaurant is the most animated scene...

Five

Boy driving a delivery wagon with new yellow mitts... A barber shop with a sign on the glass of the door: Suburbanite Shop. When you come inside, the sign is indecipherable; but look into the mirror. Same sign, Suburbanite Shop... A truck-load of old newspapers heaped into a vast mound... A truck-load of new round cotton bales... Smoke pouring out of a housetop. Somebody burning the soot out so the chimney will draw better... A wet afternoon. Youths in yellow slickers, girls with umberellas. A rose-lined parasol throws a glow over a pretty face... People driving into the traffic more impetuously than ever. Motorists careful because braking means skidding... People run to the entrance of a store, look at merchandise while they regain their breath, then run on again... Yet, everyone apparently happier in the shower. Girls smile, fellows joke. The shower is a joke, which everyone shares... It becomes a practical joke when it lasts all afternoon... In the dusk, when the lights come on, the pavement is iridescent, sometimes rainbow-coloured, like oil. Reflections of the lights sweep across the wet pavements, lights from

shops are doubled, and driving a car down a busy street
is like entering a cave of crystals... At a corner, one
looks into an art shop. There are various paintings, and
statuettes. A policeman approaches. "Now what would
ye say was the matter with that?" he asks, indicating
with a regal arm a statue of a dog with a girl on its back,
and another standing beside it. "The dog's too big. Did
you ever see a dog that came past the middle of a girl
that size? Why look at the dress of her and the braid
down her back. She must be fifteen or sixteen years of
age. That dog must be as big as a Shetland pony." He
shook his head, and returned to the corner, where he
stood watching the drops fall, and the people pass.

Six

Chilly. A sweatered teamster pulls blankets about the
necks of his horses... A well-dressed old man on Yonge
Street turns about quickly. A little girl behind him,
dodges to one side as he turns, and then to the other
when he looks there. Finally he catches sight of her,
laughing up at him; not lost at all. They go on together...
Another little girl in haphazard clothes, draws figures
in chalk of the pavement at the edge of the gutter... A
window with rubber boots, braces and bits, planes,
locks, and a pile of pennies: old coins... Huge red sign
in another: Complete Home Brew Supplies. Know What
You Drink... Two ladies entering an apartment house.

Faint perfume. They pause and call a tiny brown dog who seems to have been waiting for them on a basement window-sill... Glaringly lit bill-boards surround a smooth green-grassed expanse on three sides. In the light children play. One has a pick and is rapidly making an excavation in the sod, bringing up the brown soil... The others prance and yell, and pay no attention, though he hollers: "Going to hang a light, going to hang a red light to warn the traffic."... A long dignified old white two-storey house, with a narrow sloping-roofed piazza, its floor almost below the level of the street... A tiny square house apparently dead, but an old fine-tooled leather-bound volume holds up the window. What mystery of unrequited scholarship?... An automobile turning into a public garage at a swinging pace, without changing gears. A garage man at the doors starts back in mock terror, grinning at the driver... A bus en route: Toronto to London. Empty... A row of taxicabs approaching a theatre after the show... Jockeying for position...

Seven

A city of dogs, as well as of homes? One sees a huge dark collie gambolling on the grass before the Mining Building of the University; and at night how many men are leading dogs tiny and dogs huge, for an airing from the rooms of the apartment or the house... On the height

above Sunnyside, a portly spatted man with a cane slips
the leash from his Pom, which rolls and scrubs the grass
while he sinks to a bench… Most of the lights of
Sunnyside are gone, but they prick out, innumerable,
along the shore, stretching to points in the East and
West… A sort of little pavilion at the end of a brief pier…
Around the outside is a platform, to which are moored
skiffs and a sailboat… Always someone in the pavilion,
smoking, looking out to sea, or at the sailboats tacking to
a gap in the breakwater… The sandy beach is narrow,
then the board walk, with its occasional benches, people
walking briskly in the keen lake air… And beyond the
whizzing parkway the railroad, occasional trains, the
height with its trees and grass and benches, along King
Street… And electric signs, hugely blinding the night…
The contrast with Rosedale, houses with yellow-lit
windows, bright upper stories, or dark and sleeping…
Three cars here, and a group of people coming out, call-
ing to each other, bidding good-night in varied voices…
A taxicab driver who has just delivered a passenger,
keeping books on a paper he carries in his cap…. Cars
few and swift, rounding the large curves with a howl of
siren… Busses rumbling over bridges… An old man
with a large grey moustache and a cane, riding a
bicycle… A tiny boy with a special edition of a paper,
whose shouts might be because he is lost… Streets that
cut under Danforth… Back to East Bloor, which always
seems bare and hurried… Half-lit at night… Deserted
tea-rooms, institutional buildings, looming in the
night…

Eight

A quiet sunlit afternoon... The swoop of an automobile
down the residence street, drawing a swirl of leaves
along the asphalt, brightening in the sunlight, and
falling... A black-clothed Chinaman with a round white
bundle on his back... A woman with a dog she calls
Dimple... A traffic policeman who smiles and turns,
almost pirouetting, Master of the Revels... A sign on
Queen Street: "Tatooing done here. All the fresh
buttermilk you can drink, 5¢..." Always a crowd around
a man who writes calling cards in his own hand...
Reappearance of the first of last Winter's blue
overcoats... Richmond Street, the usual crowd about the
doors of the burlesque theatre, and two policemen who
view the opening of the show, the kicks of the chorus,
through the open doors... A store selling only locks and
keys: a potential mine of secrets... Always a crowd, and
always more than one pretty girl, waiting for cars at
Bloor and Yonge... The smell of hair and plaster and
burning, and fresh lumber, where a new building is
going up, narrowing the sidewalk... Steam from fresh
tar and cinders as the men spread it on the pavement...
A steam roller, with a man walking before it as though
heading a procession... A team of horses, not hitched to
anything, but walking with jingling harness, a man
riding one of them. The uneven clatter of their shod
hooves on the quiet street... The viaduct at Danforth.
Never many people walking the sidewalk, and never
none: a tall hustling young man in blue, a girl looking
over the parapet across the valley... Two automobiles,

each containing one man, stopped at the end of the bridge... The width of Danforth, the neat and bright array of shops, giving each an impression different from downtown. The people seem brighter and less intent... Many cheap shoe stores, and movies where you can see the picture for eleven cents... The lighting up of stores, the sudden blossoming of street lights.

Nine

In a Queen Street window, three puppies, two brown, one white, scurrying among strings of newspaper, battling, stumbling, making fierce bites at each other simultaneously, and both turning away at the same time... The red letter-box staring from Osgoode's grey front... A sweatered boy carrying a coffee-percolator... A truck-load of manure surmounted by fresh white-wooded crates... A truck bearing huge rolls of newsprint... A shop-front with windows bulging drunkenly out as though about to crash to the sidewalk... Limp old automobile tires hanging by strings, and wooden wheels of baby-buggies and express waggons hanging like neck-ornaments for giants... Two men quarrelling on a street corner. "Why, I would give my heart's blood – " the smaller says... Night. Crossing Dundas Street a topless buggy drawn by a heavy draught horse, while another is being led behind. Boys on the corner. Two men, with fresh-lit cigarettes, one

leading the other driving "Keep away, keep away boys!"
they growl, looking up and down street for traffic, and
proceeding at a walk... Dundas and Spadina: crowds of
boys dark and pale in the lights. A larger one to the rest:
"Come on gang, my little gang!"... Rain, brightening the
streets with yellow reflections of lights, darkening it with
green-blue shadows... People do not hurry, but seem to
enjoy the shower... Three children run out of a fruit-shop
ahead. One carries a stick and waves it before passersby.
The black-a-vised proprietor of the fruit-shop comes to the
door and roars after them. He is the father of the one
with the stick. "Izzie, Izzie!" laugh the other two... Sign:
Sharp Company Limited. We edge everything... A team
of horse stopped at the curb, with something long and
staringly red even in the night, behind them. The wagon
wheels are drab, and the front ones are separated from
the rear ones by twenty-five feet of freshly-painted
wooden reach. No box, no load on the waggon.

Ten

In the Ward. Front yards, where there are any, worn to
plots of mud... Pressure tanks hollowed out on one side
like canoes, for flower-boxes... Children run and
scream... In front of a drugstore, a perambulator. A little
girl rushes out of the store and begins rocking the vehicle
sideways. The infant promptly howls... Many houses
are dull-windowed, with the sign, For Sale or Rent...

Smoky brick houses, grimed white stucco over ancient
storey-and-a-half frame... Spadina Avenue. So wide you
scarcely can recognize a friend passing on the opposite
side... Cars parked along it at right angles.... Jewish
signs, Jewish papers advertised, Jewish announcements
or candidature... A shabby man examining in detail and
comparatively, two refrigerators, stamping his feet to
warm them... Snapshots enlarged in colour... The
streetcars clanging along far away in the middle of the
street, make the street seem as a wide as streets do in
advertisement photographs... A man gets off and
dodges across the traffic to the curb like a rabbit fleeing
a mown wheatfield before the binder... A church in
white brick with red stone facings.... Another church with
rosebushes about the sides, and strawy manure banked
about the roots for the Winter... A dog toddling, meets
another dog. They do not pause to salute... College
Street. New buildings, and the Reference Library against
which the ivy looks so well, as the grey limbs of trees
match the walls of the Charles Street Post-Office....
St. George Street, the park behind the library. Grass still
green, but no one on the cement seats... Stately old
houses with an air of cleanness as though the brick and
stone had been brushed yesterday. Brass plates on low
iron gates... Scholastic-looking people hurrying... A
five-tonne truck loaded with gravel, roaring and rum-
bling... A grey squirrel nibbling the grass of a lawn. He
approaches the sidewalk, but the stranger has no
peanuts to give him...

This truth...

This truth, the realization of the unity of life, and of the necessity that the heart should be the mind's Bible if a soul, as distinct from an intelligence, is to be attained, can not be shared, – it can scarcely be expressed – by abstract argument. The saying, "Beauty is truth, truth beauty, that is all ye know, and <u>all ye need to know</u>," must seem the pronouncement of futile aestheticism, or at best a perching upon a pinnacle by means of wide leaps and flights not to be discerned – unless these leaps and flights are made living and active by the form of art. In that form the appeal may be potentially universal. And the truth of poetry needs to be revealed universally. It is at the base of religion, and is one of the very few still accessible sources of religion. Our casting away of false gods has up to now resulted in the acceptance of a faith more grotesquely false – faith in civilization and betterment of conditions and mechanical adjustment. And this when as Middleton Murry says, the war wrote across the face of the heavens in letters of flame, that there is no progress save for the individual soul.

Raymond Knister in a letter to Alfred Harcourt (of Harcourt, Brace, et al.). 3.2.1930.

On Reading Aloud

It has so long been a commonplace that poetry should be read aloud, that one questions oneself rather quizzically if not seriously when the thought occurs that perhaps some poetry is not to be read aloud, or not in the way in which poetry traditionally has been read. Undoubtedly part of the charm of poetry is the music of its lines. This can scarcely be realized by silent reading. Nothing less than the actual sounding of the vowels and the feel of the rhythm will evoke fully the beauty of a noble poem. On the other hand, a just rendering of the sound values will reveal the deficiencies of a mediocre poem as nothing else will. After all poems were not made to convince us by their logic, but to move us by their music, or by the images they call up.

By their images. This is a comparatively new conception of poetry. It is perhaps a dozen or fifteen years ago that a small band of poets, some American and some English, adopted imagism, in part borrowed from the French, as a creed. This is not expressing it too strongly. The creed was precisely and definitely formulated. Nowadays all poets agree that these rules regarding the use of the exact word, the keeping of the eye on the object, and so forth, are a part of all good writing, prose and verse. But as for making the image the whole poem, that is not accepted by anyone, though many fine poems resulted from such usage.

The idea was, roughly, that each poem should comprise an image, and that this image should not be blurred by extraneous matter. You should not say that this or that was like the other; that was evading the whole issue. You were somehow to convey the identity of your bird or rock or flower or person without comparing it to something else, and without moralizing or generalizing about it.

Undoubtedly this makes for clearer and more objective, chaster art. But it is more limiting than ever the sonnet was. If each poem is to be a single image, it may be perfectly satisfying as such, and yet in many cases fail to move the reader. Seeing this most poets abandon the formula, and Ezra Pound writes: "Be in me as the eternal moods of the bleak wind, and not as transient things are, gaiety of flowers." That is a simile as much as any used by Milton or Wordsworth, both rebels in their own days. It is also as much poetry whether it is printed as prose or not.

For this movement was chiefly of free verse. It was a wholesome reaction away from the mellifluent generalities, and the obvious rhythms of the generation previous. Poetry written now is at once more restrained and more spontaneous because of it. But one wonders whether the free verse movement may not also have been an adjustment to modern conditions of reading. Comparatively seldom do people read aloud, and usually they read at such speed that the sound values of what they read are not so apparent as the images and ideas presented. Perhaps swift, plain, objective free verse is the distinctive contribution of our age to literature, and more typical of it than anything else.

Undoubtedly this kind of writing is not to be read aloud in the way that Tennyson's *Lotus Eaters*, and the poems of William Butler Yeats are to be read. "I don't act my poems," remarked one of its practitioners, with the intolerance of youth. Yet if one doubts that free verse should be read aloud let him hear, as I did, some of Carl Sandburg's poems. It is strange to find the streets and their ugliness, which all men know, converted into beauty in the soul of a man: one is moved as by the highest art, by means impossible of detection. Again, a current magazine contains a long poem called *Saint Agnes Eve in Wall Street*. It is as different from Keats' poem as the gunman and the underworld are from the gods and the Elysian fields. But it moves one to hear, spoken in impersonal and level tones, and one knows that man must go on exploring his many provinces, that his only hope is a truthful and honest search for beauty in what experience is given him, in daily life and vision.

Raymond Knister in The New Outlook *(27 October 1926).*

from **The Poetic Muse in Canada**

Our poets in Canada have been betrayed by the very richness of their material environment, so that they have depended upon their our pines and lakes more than upon their own feelings....

There have been a few exceptions. Arthur Stringer in 1914 published a book called *Open Water*, in which he reasoned admirably concerning the excusable nature of free verse, following this preface with a hundred odd pages of example. The book was politely ignored as the vagary of a too-popular novelist, but it contained more poetry than most Canadian volumes up to that time. "Autumn" and "One Night in the Northwest" are as good as most sonnets on nature by Lampman or others and they remind one of the old notion of the professional person in any line that the harder a thing is to do the more valuable it is. It is harder to walk on the tips of one's fingers, but better to walk on one's toes. Still the mood of this book is generally not intense enough for very fine poetry; and Stringer did not follow it up. Then there has been Louise Morey Bow-man, who took free verse under the best auspices. But with some exceptions she accepted it as a relaxation, or a medium for the treatment of homely, informal or queer subjects, not as the mould and making of a finer austerity, a more stringent artistry. "Sympathy" is bathos of the woman's page, "Moment Musical" an exercise in the imagistic manner. Then there has been Lawren Harris with *Contrasts*. Here we meet with a rarity: the impact of a genuine mind. Not all of the poems are poetry: the material of poetry rather, which has not been sufficiently defined and formed in art. But ["A Question"] is an example, one of the best. It combines a picture with an emotion, at least....

It need not be taken now that I am upholding free verse. I uphold poetry, which is bound to be well-done in any form. The question is, is it poetry and is it well-done? One has to answer in the negative for most of the output, metrical and ungyved of any country. But what have we accomplished?

Of late it is perceptible that a change is coming into Canadian poetry. Perhaps it began as far back as the start of Wilson MacDonald's career....

Nothing, not poetry or dreams, can exist except on the basis of reality. As long as we flinch from contact with the actual, we shall go without great poetry, and our verse will become more and more nearly dead matter.

And what hope for the future? The new poets read omnivorously, they are alive to new currents of human activity, they are not afraid of life. But the life they are given to observe is not rich in human values as that of Burns was, nor in machine values as that of Sandburg. We have Edward Sapir, who has probably written more fine metaphysical lyrics than anyone else, though he has never published a volume. Elsa Gidlow probes consciously the old mystery that enchanted Sappho. Frank Oliver Call writes sound homespun sonnets of Quebec. Francis Beatric Taylor occasionally reaches a fine integrity and spiritual passion. A.J.M. Smith sends his mind groping among concepts and emotions, of which he weaves expressionist lyrics well received in the advanced American literary periodicals. Dorothy Livesay in charmingly tacit lyrics seeks to match the ineffable word with obscure and evanescent intimations. In these people we hope.

Raymond Knister, Saturday Night, *6 October 1928*

Raymond Knister on Raymond Knister

The keynote of the literary career of Raymond Knister up to the present is experiment. This explains why it is that his place is that of a minor and little known artist in the department of belles letters in which he has dabbled. Among the writers in the English speaking countries it is an open secret that he is a person of potentialities and even belief. But the general public has scarcely heard his name. It would have been almost a physical impossibility to have produced a body of work in poetry, drama, the short story, and the novel, sufficient to have impressed critical powers, at the age of thirtytwo. And it would have been still more difficult to do those things and at the same time keep contributing miscellaneous matter to current magazines. Of all the experimenting Knister has indulged himself with, that of making a living by ephemeral pot-boiling is probably the most detrimental to his progress as an artist. Yet in his detached and experimental attitude toward writing is to be found one of the most hopeful auguries of the future.

It was ten years ago that Knister's first short story was published, "The One Thing," in *The Midland* for January 1922, while a group of *Several Poems* appeared in the same magazine for December. At this time H.L. Mencken was declaring that *The Midland*, a tiny periodical with small circulation, was the most important magazine ever founded in America, which is to be explained by the fact that it was the only authentic indigenous group expression of the region regarded as the most important in America. It will help us to assess the contribution of this writer if we consider him from this point of view. For here almost if not quite for the first time, we find Canadian farm life depicted with faithfulness and warmth, with a realism which is almost too literal. Consider "Feed," which though it was written with some care for sound-values as well as those of thought, could not conceivably have been printed by a Canadian editor in 1922 [see page 11].

The reader of Canadian poetry would have found the poem laughable from its choice of subject matter, notwithstanding the fact that the continuity of life and experience had been expressed long before by mystic and bard; while of course the form would have appeared to be "shredded prose." It was in the use of language that this farm boy broke with the respectable mode in Canadian literature. There had been so much meretricious mellifluence passing for poetry that he delighted in eschewing metaphor and simile, in putting down lines which placed the object itself within the reader's ken, without the aid of adventitious trapping:

As in other times the trees stand tense and lonely
And spread a hollow moan of other times.

Language was used as a medium for the expression of something which formed pictures of a kind of life peculiar to the writer's own experience, and so, paradoxically, it became something possessing weight and value in its own right:

There is only the creak of harness
And the low words of teamsters
In the unplanted fields,
And in the field where the roller is
There shall be no more loudness
Until the wind rasps dried stalks

> *And boys shout to each other*
> *Above the crisp surf-noise,*
> *Among the gold mounds of corn*
> *Stretching in rows.*

Enough of these poems appeared in American poetry journals to form a small volume — though their author would not consent to publish at his own expense — a volume which would have possessed considerable value in the formation of a national consciousness, and might have had more influence than they had in encouraging the assertion of other talents.

In these attempts as in the short stories, there was more of traditionalism than fashion. As a boy Knister had studied Goethe, Homer, Dante, translating Moliere and Flaubert for his own amusement at fifteen. That first short story is reminiscent of Flaubert in so far as form went, though the prose was so unsatisfactory that he rewrote it after publication. It dealt with the life of a queer little farmer and an overmastering obsession, and while tragedy was the outcome, the chief technical effect was the rendering of the passage of many years in a few short pages. A number of these stories, in the course of time, found their way into print, were bestarred or anthologized, or listed by the *Bookman* (New York) among the ten best of the year. But meanwhile, the writer turned to other things.

After a year of thought given to the form of the novel, he considered that he had arrived at a new mold for his material — farm life in Ontario — and wrote a seventy-thousand word novel in eleven days. This, critics who read it claim, represents some of his best work, and it is to be hoped that he will give it the rounding out which will permit publication. Also he began to review books regularly in the local paper, the *Border Cities Star*, and continued for two or three years in the pungent expression of opinions which were soon quoted widely. At the same time he was working on the editorial staff of *The Midland* in Iowa City, and coming into contact with sympathetic minds and ambitions: no less than five books which were published later were being written by men in that office. Ruth Suckow had hold of the position of assistant editor the year before. He drafted another novel, with which he was even more dissatisfied than with the first. He had written one play – a tragedy of course, which eventually was published in *Poet Lore* (Boston), in the Winter of 1928. It was called *Youth Goes West*, and dealt with the farm boy's immemorial desire for wider horizons.

In Chicago, after his year on *The Midland*, he gained in a few months a fund of experience of life in what is called the seamy side, trying various jobs as distinct from positions. Then back to the farm again. Ernest Walsh and Ethel Moorhead advertised a new magazine they were about to publish in Paris. Raymond Knister sent a story, and soon saw his name on the cover of *This Quarter* with those of Ezra Pound, James Joyce, Carl Sandburg, and Ernest Hemingway. A subsequent issue, which included Morley Callaghan's first published story, contained a story and a dozen poems which *The New Criterion* (London) singled out for special praise for their freshness and objectivity.

At about this time Canadian magazines began to get into touch with Knister, and he moved to Toronto, there to make at freelance writing. He had long felt the need for some encouragement for Canadian writers, and not having money to found a magazine, persuaded a publisher to let him edit *Canadian Short Stories*.

This brings us up to the time of our author's first published novel, *White Narcissus*, which had been drafted years before on the farm, as an experiment in a *genre*. Here we find the strict objectivity of the early stories and poems relaxed in favour of the adoption of a sty, and while the style had a sufficient measure of distinction to win the backing of publishers of repute in three counties, it can not be claimed that the book was an outstanding success. While the reviewers in the *Manchester Guardian* and metropolitan American papers gave it lengthy and respectful consideration mainly on account of this style, Canadian critics were disappointed by a lack of sociological import and local colour, or rather by the use given the latter. The fact is that *White Narcissus* is one of the most artistically planned novels we have had, but it lacks a "significant" theme; its material is slight. Richard Milne, the protagonist, is a writer, a city man returning to the country and to his old love. The situation is psychologically complicated by the fact of the heroine's forced attachment to her parents, who have never spoken to one another in her experience; almost nothing is made of the mother's attachment to the narcissi as a symbol, in the psychiatrist's jargon. Moreover, while farm life and manners are identifiable and immediate, they are viewed through the coloured spectacles of a temperament, and a prevailing mood; and while the device of causing the hero to "throw back" and become part of his form life so as to give the scene its proper foundation is admirable, as securing unity and setting the story on a solid foundation, the story itself leaves something to be desired. It is, first and last, the heroine's story; Richard Milne is only the quasi-protagonist. And while it is an unambitious tale to which, as critics agreed, the happy ending was the natural one, the atmosphere of the beginning seems slightly too charged, while the ending tapers off too rapidly. Notwithstanding this and the fact that *White Narcissus* gives somewhat the air of being a *tour-de-force*, it may be accepted as a first novel of distinction.

This article was written by Raymond Knister in 1932. To assist Leo Kennedy in profiling Knister for The Canadian Forum.

Knister Chronology

Chronology of Raymond Knister's Poetic Career

1899: 27 May: John Raymond Knister born in Ruscomb, near Windsor in Essex County, Ontario.

1918: 10 January: "A New Year's Reverie" published in *The Farmer's Almanac*. 1920: March: "La Vie" published in *The Rebel*.

1921: Collects his best poems under the title *Grass * Plaitings*.

1922: Went to Chicago. December: "Lake Harvest," "Feed," "Change," "Snowfall," "Stable-Talk," "February's Forgotten Mitts," "Peach Buds," published in *The Midland*.

1923: May-June: "Boy Remembers in the Field" published in *Voices*. October: "Reverie: The Orchard on the Slope," "October Stars" published in *The Midland*.

1924: April: "The Hawk" published in *Poetry*. May: "Night Walk," "The Roller," "In the Rain, Sowing Oats," "White Cat," "The Ploughman" published in *The Midland*. 24 September: Leaves Chicago for Canada. October: Writes "After Exile" and "A Row of Horse Stalls."

1925: 25 January: Appointed Canadian correspondent for *This Quarter*. April: "Dog and Cat" and "Martyrdom" published in *The Midland*. October: Publishes "After Exile" in *Voices*. Manuscript of selected poems *Windfalls for Cider* sent to Lorne Pierce. "*A Row of Stalls*" published in *This Quarter*.

1926: "The Ploughman's Song" published in *The Buccaneer*.

1927: March: Lectures on Duncan Campbell Scott at the University of Toronto 1932: 10 August: Hired as Assistant Editor for the Ryerson Press. 29 August: Drowns at age 33 at Stoney Point, Ontario. September: "Lake Harvest," "Change," "Stable-Talk," "The Roller," "The White Cat," "The Ploughman," "October Stars," "The Hawk," "Boy Remembers in the Field" published in *The Canadian Forum*.

1949: *Collected Poems*, Ed. Dorothy Livesay, publishes "A Road," "Child Dreams," "The Colt," "On a Skyscraper," "Ambition," "Bees," "Poisons," "Haunted House," "Reply to August," "Moments When I'm Feeling Poems," "Wind's Way," "Autumn

Clouds," "Quiet Snow," and "Forward to *Windfalls for Cider*" for first time.

1975: *Raymond Knister: Poems, Stories, and Essays,* ed. David Arnason, publishes "Over Trees and Spring Dusk," "Arab King," "Time," "Full Moon," "Spring-flooded Ditches," "An Old Wooden Windmill," "Cliff" and "Maud & Jess" from *A Row of Stalls,* "Consummation," "So Long Lives This," "Whip-Poor-Will in North Woods," "Woman Reading Poetry," and "Against the Yearsby'" for first time.

1982: *Canadian Poetry 1,* Ed. David Lecker, publishes "Sumach" and "The Humourist" for first time.

1983: *Windfalls for Cider… The Poems of Raymond Knister,* Ed. Joy Kuropatwa publishes "Cedars," "Elm-Tree and Sun," "The Motor: A Fragment," "Possession," "Corn Husking," "Sea-Blue Eyes," "Speculation in a Flower Market," "Dilettante," "Immemorial Plea," "March Wind," "Night Whistling," "The Quick and the Dead," "Superfluous Words on a Drive," "Cinquain: Pattern," "Because They Are Young" for first time.

2002: September: *Exile Quarterly* publishes "The Life in Letters (Parts 1 thru 3)," "East Side," "The Longest June Evening," "In a Conservatory," "Now Me," "Conundrum," "Dragonflies at Noon," "For One Quick" for first time.

Previously Unpublished Poems:

"The Spirit of War," "The Wind," "The Quester Rewarded," "Frost in Childhood," "Enemies," "From a Train: Slums and Fields," "The Life in Letters (Part IV)," "A Face in a Motor," "Minutiae," "Parting on the Beach," "Fall-time Milking," "Nellie Rackerfield," "Madrigal," "Quarry," "Sonnet: A Soldier," "Spring-Flooded Ditches," "The Unattainable," "To One Lost," "Lachrymae Rerum," "Did We Need the Rain," "Liberty Nut-Cracker No.1," "Liberty Nut-Cracker No.2," "Serene, mounting as a bird's far cry," "To J.A.C. On Receipt of a Portrait," "A Foiled Coquette," "In the Spring Dusk, Gazing Above the Trees," "Yet Again," "Until, Still Young," "There is no sleep but tossing," "Dream," "August Night," "And is it to remember."

Raymond Knister in Poetry Anthologies

In Chronological Order

Anthology of Canadian Poetry (English). Ralph Gustafson.
    Middlesex: Penguin, 1942.
Collected Poems of Raymond Knister. Dorothy Livesay.
    Toronto: Ryerson Press, 1949.
Canadian Poems: 1850-1952. Louis Dudek and Irving Layton.
    Toronto: Contact Press, 1953.
The Book of Canadian Poetry: A Critical and Historical Anthology.
    A.J.M. Smith.
    Toronto: Gage, 1957.
Penguin Book of Canadian Verse. Ralph Gustafson.
    Middlesex: Penguin Books, 1958, 1967, 1970, 1975, 1980 and
    1984.
The Oxford Book of Canadian Verse in English and French. A.J.M.
    Smith.
    Toronto: Oxford University Press, 1960, 1961 and 1968.
A Book of Canadian Poems: An Anthology for Secondary School.
    Carlyle King.
    Toronto: McClelland&Stewart, 1963.
Forum: Canadian Life and Letters 1920-70. J.L. Granastein and Peter
    Stevens.
    Toronto: University of Toronto Press, 1972.
The Evolution of Canadian Literature in English. Vol. 3. Mary Jane
    Edwards, George Parker, and Paul Denham.
    Toronto: Holt, Rinehart, and Winston, 1973
Poems, Stories, and Essays. Ed. John Moss, David Arnason and
    John Sorfleet.
    Montreal: Bellock Press, 1975.
A Centruy of Canadian Verse. H. Gordon Green.
    Toronto: Ryerson, 1967.
The Poets of Canada. John R. Colombo.
    Edmonton: Hurtig, 1978.

Literature in Canada. Vol. 2. Douglas Daymond and Leslie
  Monkman.
  Toronto: Gage Education, 1978.
To Say the Least: Canadian Poets from A to Z. P.K. Page.
  Toronto: Press Porcepic, 1979.
The Poetry of Horses. Samuel Carr.
  London: B.T. Bastford, 1980.
Canadian Poetry. Vol. 1. Jack David and Robert Lecker.
  Toronto: General and EGW, 1982
The New Oxford Book of Canadian Verse in English. Margaret
  Atwood.
  Toronto: Oxford University Press, 1982 and 1983.
Poetry in Focus. Bob Cameron, et al.
  Toronto: Globe/Modern Curriculum, 1983.
Windfalls for Cider... The Poems of Raymond Knister. Joy
  Kuropatwa.
  Windsor: Black Moss, 1983.
Following the Plough. John B. Lee.
  Windsor: Black Moss, 2000.
The Penguin Treasury of Popular Canadian Poems and Song. John
Colombo.
  Toronto: Penguin, 2002.

Works Cited and Consulted

Arnason, David. "Canadian Poetry: The Interregnum." *CV/II*. 1.1. (Spring 1975). 28-32.

Beattie, Munro. "Poetry 1920-1935." *Literary History of Canada: Canadian Literature in English*. 2nd edition. Ed. Carl Klinck. Toronto: University of Toronto Press, 1976. 239-41.

Bohan, Ruth. *The Société Anonyme's Brooklyn Exhibition*. Ann Arbor: UMI Research Press, 1982.

Brooker, Bertram. *Think of the Earth*.
Toronto: Thomas Nelson, 1936.
"When We Rise!" *Yearbook of the Arts in Canada, 1928-1929*.
Ed. Bertram Brooker.
Toronto: Macmillan, 1929.

Burke, Anne. "Raymond Knister: An Annotated Bibliography." *Essays in Canadian Writing*. *16* (Fall-Winter 1979-80).
Catalogue of the International Exhibition of Modern Art: Assembled by the Société Anonyme (Toronto: Art Gallery of Toronto, 1927).

Eggleston, Wilfrid. *Literary Friends*.
Borealis Press, Ottawa 1980.

Givens, Imogen. "Raymond Knister – Man or Myth?" *Essays In Canadian Writing*. 16 (Fall-Winter 1979-80). 5-19.
"Addresses." Unpublished.
Afterword. *Windfalls for Cider... The Poems of Raymond Knister*.
Windsor: Black Moss Press, 1983.

Harris, Lawren. "Revelation of Art in Canada." Canadian Theosophist. 7 (15 July 1926). 85-8.

Kennedy, Leo. "Raymond Knister." *The Canadian Forum:* XXI (September, 1932). 459-66.

Keith, W.J. *Literary Images of Ontario*.
Toronto: University of Toronto Press, 1992.

Kizuk, Alexander. *A Reassessment of Early Twentieth-Century Canadian Poetry in English*.
Queenston: Edwin Mellen Press, 2000.
Knister, Raymond. "Canadian Letter." *The First Day of Spring: Stories and Other Prose*. Ed. Peter Stevens.
Toronto: University of Toronto Press, 1976.
  Introduction. *Canadian Short Stories*. Edited by Raymond Knister.
Toronto: MacMillan, 1928.
  Letters. William Ready Archives (McMaster University).
Kuropatwa, Joy. Introduction. *Windfalls for Cider... The Poems of Raymond Knister*. Ed. by Joy Kuropatwa. Preface by James Reaney. Afterword by Imogen Knister Grace.
Windsor: Black Moss Press, 1983.
Kuropatwa, Joy. *Raymond Knister and His Works*.
Toronto: ECW Press, 1987.
Lecker, Robert. *Making It Real: The Canonization of English-Canadian Literature*.
Toronto: Anansi, 1995.
Lennox, John and Clara Thomas. *William Arthur Deacon: A Literary Life*.
Toronto: University of Toronto Press, 1982.
Livesay, Dorothy. Memoir. *Collected Poems of Raymond Knister*. Ed. Dorothy Livesay.
Toronto: Ryerson Press, 1949.
O'Halloran, Bonita. "Chronological History of Raymond Knister." *Journal of Canadian Fiction*. 14 (1975). 194-99.
Pacey, Desmond. Introduction. *The Letters of Frederick Philip Grove*.
Toronto: University of Toronto Press, 1976.
Pantazzi, Sybille. "Foreign Art at the Canadian National Exhibition 1905-1938." National Gallery of Canada Annual Bulletin 22 (1973).

Precosky, Don. "Ever With Discontent: Some Comments on
    Raymond Knister and His Poetry." *CV/II*. 4.4
    (Spring 1980). 3-9.
Read, Herbert. "Exiles." Review of *This Quarter*. *The New
    Criterion*. 2 (April 1926). 403-4.
Stevens, Peter. "The Old Futility of Art: Knister's Poetry."
    Canadian Literature. 23 (Winter 1965). 45-52.
Stevens, Peter. Introduction. *The First Day of Spring: Stories and
    Other Prose*. Literature of Canada: Poetry and Prose in Reprint,
    No 17.
    Toronto: University of Toronto Press, 1976.
Voaden, Herman. "Earth Song." *Earth Song*.
    Toronto: Playwrights Co-op, 1976.
—. "Creed for a New Theatre: 'Symphonic Expressionism', a
    Composite Blending of All Theatral Arts Explained in
    Detail as a Possible Stage Method for the Future," *Toronto
    Globe*, December 17, 1932.
Waddington, Marcus. "Raymond Knister: A Biographical
    Note." *Journal of Canadian Fiction*. 14
    (1975). 175-92.
—. *Raymond Knister and The Canadian Short Story*. PhD
    Dissertation. Carleton University, 1977.
Whiteman, Bruce. Editor. *A Literary Friendship: The
    Correspondence of Ralph Gustafson and W.W.E. Ross*.
    Toronto: ECW Press, 1984.
Wood, John and Allan Anderson. Producers. *The Poet Who Was
    a Farmer Too: A Profile of Raymond Knister*.
    CBC Radio. 19 July 1964.

Related Reading

Anthologies:

Canadian Poetry 1920 to 1960. Ed. Brian Trehearne.
   Toronto: McClelland & Stewart, 2010.
The Book of Canadian Poetry: A Critical and Historical Anthology.
   Ed. A.J.M. Smith.
   Toronto: W.J. Gage, 1943.
Yearbook of the Arts in Canada 1928-1929. Ed. Bertram Brooker.
   Toronto: Macmillan, 1929.
Yearbook of the Arts in Canada 1936. Ed. Bertram Brooker.
   Toronto: Macmillan, 1936.

Memoirs and Analysis of the Period:

*Canada's Lost Plays: The Developing Mosaic: English-Canadian
   Drama to Mid-Century*. Ed. Anton Wagner.
   Downsview: Canadian Theatre Review, 1980.
The Canadian Modernists Meet. Ed. Dean Irvine.
   Ottawa: University of Ottawa Press, 2005. 181-204.
Beattie, Munro. "Poetry 1920-1935." *Literary History of Canada:
   Canadian Literature in English*. Ed. Carl F. Klinck.
   Toronto: University of Toronto Press, 1976.
Betts, Gregory. "Before Our Time: Radical English-Canadian
   Poetries Across the Post/Modern Divide."
   Canadian Poetry. 60 (Spring-Summer 2007). 22-45.
Carr, Emily. "Hundreds of Thousands: The Journals of an
   Artist." *The Complete Writings of Emily Carr*.
   Toronto: University of Washington Press, 1993. 653-893.
Davis, Ann. *The Logic of Ecstasy: Canadian Mystical Painting
   1920-1940*.
   Toronto: University of Toronto Press, 1992.
Dudek, Louis and Michael Gnarowski. *The Making of Modern
   Poetry in Canada: Essential Articles on Contemporary
   Canadian Poetry in English*.
   Toronto: Ryerson Press, 1962.

Eggleston, Wilfrid. *Literary Friends.*
    Ottawa: Borealis Press, 1980.
Finlay, Karen A. *The Force of Culture: Vincent Massey and
    Canadian Sovereignty.*
    Toronto: University of Toronto Press, 2004.
Hill, Colin. *Modern Realism in English-Canadian Fiction.*
    Toronto: University of Toronto Press, 2011.
Irvine, Dean. *Editing Modernity: Women and Little-Magazine
    Cultures in Canada. 1916-1956.*
    Toronto: University of Toronto Press, 2008.
Kizuk, Alexander. *A Reassessment of Early Twentieth-Century
    Canadian Poetry in English.*
    Queenston: Edwin Mellen Press, 2000.
Lennox, John and Clara Thomas. *William Arthur Deacon: A
    Canadian Literary Life.*
    Toronto: University of Toronto Press, 1982.
Norris, Ken. *The Little Magazine in Canada 1925-80.*
    Toronto: ECW Press, 1984.
Trehearne, Brian. *Aestheticism and the Canadian Modernists:
    Aspects of a Poetic Influence.*
    Montreal: McGill-Queen's Press, 1989.
Livesay, Dorothy. *Right Hand Left Hand: A True Life of the
    Thirties.*
    Erin: Press Porcepic, 1977.
McKay, Ian. *Reasoning Otherwise: Leftists and the People's
    Enlightenment in Canada, 1890-1920.*
    Toronto: Between the Lines, 2008.
Stevenson, Lionel. *Appraisals of Canadian Literature.*
    Toronto: Macmillan, 1926.

Related Poetry and Fiction Titles from the Period:
Bowman, Louise Morey. *Characters in Cadence.*
    Toronto: Macmillan, 1938.
Brooker, Bertram. *The Wrong World: Selected Stories and Essays.*
    Ottawa: University of Ottawa Press, 2009.

—. *Think of the Earth*. 1936.
    Toronto: Brown Bear Press, 2000.
Callaghan, Morley. *Strange Fugitive*. Exile Classics Series No. 19.
    Exile Editions, 2011.
de la Roche, Mazo. *Selected Stories*.
    Ottawa : University of Ottawa Press, 1979.
Grove, Frederick Philip. *Settlers of the Marsh*.
    Toronto: Ryerson Press, 1925.
Harris, Lawren. *In the Ward: His Urban Poetry and Painting*. Ed.
    Gregory Betts.
    Toronto: Exile Editions, 2007.
MacDonald, Wilson. *Out of the Wilderness*.
    Ottawa: Graphic Publishers, 1926.
Ostenso, Martha. *Wild Geese. 1925*.
    Toronto: McClelland & Stewart, 1989.
Livesay, Dorothy, *Right hand, Left hand*.
    Erin: Press Porcepic, 1977.
Ross, W.W.E. *Irrealities, Sonnets & Laconics*. Eds. Gregory Betts
    and Barry Callaghan.
    Toronto: Exile Editions, 2003.
Stringer, Arthur. *Open Water*.
    New York: John Lane, 1914.

Questions For Discussion And Essays

Introduction

1. Knister's vision for an ideal Canadian literary magazine was "Canadianism at all costs." What did he mean by this? How does it relate to his international publishing experiences?

2. What factors limited the opportunities for Canadian writers during this period?

3. After Knister's death, Leo Kennedy said that Knister "was on his way up." What evidence was there for this? How significant is Knister's literary success during this period?

4. How important is his early death in the story of Raymond Knister? Is it valuable to compare him to John Keats?

5. Why do you think he returned to Canada? What risks were involved? What was to be gained?

Grass * Plaitings

1. How does the mood shift with each season in "A Road"? What do people use the road for?

2. "Cedars" uses personification in its depiction of the landscape. What human characteristics does Knister give to the trees? How do the humans in the second stanza connect to the trees in the first stanza?

3. Who is the speaker in "Peach Buds"? What is the speaker waiting for?

4. Where does the speaker find "The Spirit of War"? What does she do?

5. How does the first stanza relate to the second stanza in "Reverie: The Orchard on the Slope"?

6. In "Enemies," what is the "It" that the playwright had thought of?

7. What king of a creature is the "Arab King"? Why do you think he doesn't race?

8. Compare "From a Train: Slums and Fields" to "After Exile." How is the perspective different? How is it the same?

9. What metaphors or symbols does Knister use in each section of "The Life in Letters"? How do these connect to the title of each section?

10. "A Face in a Motor" and "On a Skyscraper" both depict life in the modern world. What effect do the new technologies and buildings have on human relationships?

11. What is "The Roller"? What alchemy shall it work?

12. Why does it give him "joy" to pass the things that he does in "The Motor: A Fragment"?

13. What is the mood in "East Side"? What is the "old thought" that haunts old Joachim?

14. What gives "The Ploughman" discontent? How does this poem compare to "Ploughman's Song"?

15. What is the substance being sprayed in "Poisons"? What does it remind Gil Alberts of?

16. How does the perspective change with each stanza in "The Hawk"?

17. How and why do Roy and the speaker's father tease Bill during "Corn Husking"?

Windfalls for Cider (1925)

1. In his Foreword to *Windfalls for Cider*, Knister argues against "sonorous phrases." What are his reasons, and what does he hope avoiding this tendency will produce?

2. In "After Exile," the speaker says that "It is not at no cost I see it all." What does he see? What is the cost?

3. How does the speaker relate to the landscape that he surveys? Why does he think himself "wise" to see it pass in the last line of the poem?

4. In his explanation of the poem sequence "A Row of Stalls," Knister claims that "The art which conceals art seems to me best." How does this series of poems fulfill that ambition?

5. Explain the shift in the last line of "Consummation."

6. What does poetry feel like according to "Moments When I'm Feeling Poems"?

7. How is "March Wind" a 'fallacy set to music'?

On Raymond Knister

1. The letters collected in this book help to document the impact and reputation of Raymond Knister at the time of his premature death. What aspects of his career and talent do these letters eulogize?

2. Having read his published poetry now, what are some things that you have observed that these letters overlook?

Poems, Stories, and Essays

1. "A New Year's Reverie" uses a much more traditional form than Knister's other poems. Why is the older form appropriate for the content of this poem?

2. How does "Against the Years" characterize other early modern writers?

Windfalls for Cider (1983)

1. Why does "The Humorist" feel disappointed in his career?

2. Why do "they" hate "you" in "The Quick and the Dead"?

Unpublished Poetry

1. Compare the alternate versions of poems and consider the significance and the reasons for the changes.

2. Read Morley Callaghan's description of Knister and then consider what might be the significance of the repetition in "Dragonflies at Noon."

3. What does the rain "tell" of in "Did We Need theRain"?

4. What is the fabric in "Pattern: Fabric."

5. What stops the speaker from dreaming in "Yet Again"? Does he regret this loss?

6. Why cannot Love grow old in "And is it to remember"?

A New Heaven and A New Earth

1. What kind of details attract the narrator's attention in "Sidewalks of Toronto"? What kind of impression do these details give of the city?

2. How does Knister correct the famous Keats quote in "This Truth"?

3. According to "On Reading Aloud," what special insights can one glean by reading a poem out loud?

Major Themes and Symbols

Automobiles
Toil
Perspective
Horses
Farm life
Trains and travel
Love
Relationships
Exile

General Questions

1. Toronto had a vibrant modernist arts culture in the 1920s that Knister participated in. Even though Knister is primarily heralded as a rural poet, where does the city appear in his work? What do the appearances of urban life suggest about his opinion of the city?

2. What role does the First World War play in Knister's writing?

3. In what way was Knister "in exile" when he left Canada? In what way did he remain in exile after returning?

4. Find all of the characters that appear in Knister's poetry. What are the speaker's relationships to these people? Why do more characters get names on the farm than in the city?

5. How much has Canadian farming changed since Knister's time? How much has stayed the same?

6. Based on what details fascinated Knister about the Canadian farm, how do you think he would feel about contemporary industrial models of farming?

Of Interest on the Web

Burke, Anne. "Some Annotated Letters of A.J.M. Smith and Raymond Knister."
http://www.uwo.ca/english/canadianpoetry/cpjrn/vol11/burke.htm

Online Guide to Canadian Writing: contains a wide array of links and information on Canadian authors.
http://www.track0.com/ogwc/